Changing the Course of Failure

Changing the Course of Failure

How Schools and Parents Can Help Low-Achieving Students

Sandra Stotsky

ROWMAN & LITTLEFIELD
Lanham • Boulder • New York • London

Published by Rowman & Littlefield
An imprint of The Rowman & Littlefield Publishing Group, Inc.
4501 Forbes Boulevard, Suite 200, Lanham, Maryland 20706
www.rowman.com

Unit A, Whitacre Mews, 26-34 Stannary Street, London SE11 4AB

Copyright © 2018 by The Rowman & Littlefield Publishing Group, Inc.

All rights reserved. No part of this book may be reproduced in any form or by any electronic or mechanical means, including information storage and retrieval systems, without written permission from the publisher, except by a reviewer who may quote passages in a review.

British Library Cataloguing in Publication Information Available

Library of Congress Cataloging-in-Publication Data Available
Library of Congress Control Number: 2018938141

ISBN 978-1-4758-3995-1 (cloth : alk. paper)
ISBN 978-1-4758-3996-8 (pbk. : alk. paper)
ISBN 978-1-4758-3997-5 (electronic)

∞ ™ The paper used in this publication meets the minimum requirements of American National Standard for Information Sciences Permanence of Paper for Printed Library Materials, ANSI/NISO Z39.48-1992.

Printed in the United States of America

To my five children and many grandchildren

Contents

Acknowledgments		xi
Preface: Teachers are not Substitutes for Families—or Accountable for Low Achievement		xiii
Notes		xvii
1	The Current Education Problem	1
	Beginning of Direct Federal Involvement in Local Public Education	2
	Concluding Remarks	8
	Key Ideas to Remember	9
	Notes	9
2	The Current Political Context for the Education of Low-Achieving Students	13
	Every Student Succeeds Act of December 2015	13
	Changes in the Purpose of the Elementary and Secondary Education Act	15
	How to Address Undefined Equal Outcomes Not Caused by the Education System?	16
	Key Ideas to Remember	16
	Notes	17
3	Early U.S. Educational History	19
	Pre–World War II K–12 Education	20
	Development of the "Comprehensive" High School	20
	Awareness of High School Weaknesses	22
	Key Ideas to Remember	23
	Notes	24
4	Fragmentation of the English Curriculum in the Twentieth Century	25
	Structural Changes in K–12 Education at the Turn of the Twentieth Century	26
	Fragmentation of a Coherent Secondary Literature Curriculum	30
	Further Weakening of a Coherent English Curriculum	35
	Key Ideas to Remember	37
	Notes	37

5	Evolving Explanations of Low Achievement: How Well Education Programs and Strategies Have Addressed It	41
	"Factors Contributing to Achievement Gaps" According to the NEA	41
	Strategies or Programs to Address Low Achievement	44
	Key Ideas to Remember	53
	Notes	54
6	Who Should Teach Low-Achieving Students—and All the Others?	59
	What Is Teacher Quality?	59
	What Is the Academic Quality of the Teaching Force?	60
	The Major Obstacle in Strengthening Teacher Quality	62
	Origins and Evolution of Teacher Quality Controls	62
	Quality of Undergraduate Teacher Preparation Programs	65
	Diversity or Quality in K–12 Teachers	66
	Speaking Up for Quality First	68
	Concluding Remarks	69
	Key Ideas to Remember	70
	Notes	70
7	Testing Concerns	73
	Teacher Concerns	73
	Parent Concerns	76
	Key Ideas to Remember	78
	Notes	79
8	What Might Desperate Education Policy Makers Do?	81
	Why New Ideas Are Needed	81
	Why Some of the Latest Ideas Are Unlikely to Work	84
	Notes	87
9	What Can State Legislatures with a Spine Do?: Possibilities	89
	High Costs and Little Return on the Investment	89
	What State Legislatures Can Do, With or Without Federal Permission	92
	Large-Scale Programs with Evidence	96
	Possible Long-Term Solutions to Massive Adolescent Underachievement	96
	Notes	98
10	Policies to Reduce Adolescent Underachievement or High School Dropouts	101
	Five Education-Oriented Policies	101
	A Non-Education Approach to a Non-Teacher-Caused Problem	107
	Notes	108

About the Author 111

Acknowledgments

To the many other parents and grandparents across this country who want their public schools to prepare their children and grandchildren for the demanding but voluntary activities of self-government.

Preface

Teachers are not Substitutes for Families—or Accountable for Low Achievement

This book is about this country's efforts to educate and raise the achievement level of large numbers of low-achieving students—students who perform academically below average for their age or grade level. It suggests alternatives to what educators over the past century and a half have done (especially in reading or English classes) to keep large groups of low-achieving students in school until high school graduation.

This book is not just about the education of students with low-income parents. All low-achieving students do not have low-income or poorly-educated parents. (Nor do all low-income parents have low-achieving children.) This book is about students who are not eligible to become members of their high school's Honor Society when in high school and who usually need developmental coursework (below-college-level coursework) in mathematics and reading if they are admitted to college. But they or their parents are not necessarily poor.

This country has always had low-achieving students (relatively-speaking) and always will. Every country has and will continue to have low-achieving students. Because low achievement anywhere is relative to high achievement, there will always be low-achieving students. However, efforts to educate low-achievers in this country today are more difficult than they should be because low achievers are not considered responsible for their low achievement. Their schools, teachers, even parents are. And because low achievers are not held accountable in any way for their academic efforts, they have no reason to change their academic behavior or academic status. They get the rewards higher-achievers once did without having to exert the academic effort higher-achievers once did.

There are several reasons why low-achieving students are at the center of educational attention today. (1) Many of them in this country are African Americans or have dark complexions and poor parents. Americans in general have been taught that they are responsible for these low-achieving students chiefly because of the attitudes and behaviors of their ancestors towards people or immigrants who didn't look, talk, or act like them.

(2) Whatever their background, there's little evidence that low achievers on average read or write better than they did decades ago despite all the money and programs devoted to their education in the past fifty years.

(3) Large differences in academic achievement across politically defined groups are considered unacceptable by education policy makers and many others today.[1] These differences are considered *today* a reflection of an unequal allocation of resources such as school facilities, teachers, and curriculum materials across public schools.

The basic purpose of this book is to raise several questions in readers' minds:

1. First, what can help education policy makers to understand that widespread adolescent under-achievement is a social problem and not susceptible to solution by educational interventions no matter how much money is allocated to public schools and colleges?
2. Second, what kinds of evidence do education policy makers need to understand that it damages all students' education to expect the wrong institutions (public schools and colleges) to keep on trying to solve a growing social problem?
3. Finally, what are the varied civic costs of this country's institutionally misplaced focus on low achievement?

These questions become urgent when a U.S. Department of Education-funded study of a community college issued in April 2017 finds that most fulltime first-time freshmen seeking an associate degree were initially placed in developmental [below college-level] courses in English and in math. In other words, most students were unprepared for college coursework,[2] raising questions about the best uses of post-secondary resources and the effectiveness of K-12 education resources.

Many education policy makers seem to think that all Hispanic and African American students are low achievers. But only 25 percent of this country's fifteen year-olds are low achievers, according to the 2012 Program for International Student Assessment (PISA) results,[3] the same percentage of grade 8 students in the 2015 National Assessment of Educational Progress (NAEP) reading test who were "below Basic" in Reading.[4] Since Hispanic and African American children constituted 41 percent of our public school population in 2016,[5] many perhaps most are not low achievers according to test results.

Many education policy makers also seem to think that that most of the children in poor or low-income families are Hispanic or African American. But that is not the case with respect to numbers. The National Center for Children in Poverty at Columbia University finds more "white" children in low-income families than any other racial group.[6] The percentage of each group in low-income families may be higher for Hispanic or African American children, but not the overall numbers. Policy makers want "gaps" closed between the members of these two groups and other non-Asian groups in this country without clarifying what is meant by a gap.

Puzzlingly, growing academic differences between "Asian" students and "white," Hispanic, or African American students raise few if any expressions of concern by education policy makers. Moreover, many policy makers have chosen to see academic differences among *only* non-Asian student groups as unacceptable. They have also chosen to see these differences chiefly as a reflection of an unequal allocation of such educational resources as school facilities, teachers, and curriculum materials, or of unequal "access" to them.[7] And many have chosen to attribute what they see as an unequal allocation of resources to bigotry in our local communities and in educators themselves (e.g., the "stress of racism on learning").[8]

These choices by policy makers have created at least two problems. By claiming bigotry as a cause of the gaps, they have implied that local educators are accountable for the gaps. This claim also seems to have led policy makers to develop weak (gap-closing) English language arts standards, not academically strong standards, to guide development of the K-12 classroom curriculum and teachers' professional development. Weak standards may have been created based on the assumption that most low achievers couldn't address academically strong standards.

As a corollary to the charge, implicit or not, that local communities and the educators they hire are bigoted, many education policy makers and their supporters have aimed to increase centralization of education policies in the federal government. Using federal money to the states as the carrot, they have sought to shape or control the distribution of educational resources in ways these policy makers believe or claim is equitable.[9]

Policy makers have expressed no faith in local communities or the educators they hired to establish and implement policies seen as equitable. Why would they, if local communities and the educators they hire are perceived as bigots? Hence, the publicly unknown writers of the Every Student Succeeds Act (ESSA) required four-year education plans for the entire state to be approved by the U.S. Department of Education (USED), not by local school boards, parent groups, state legislatures, or even governors.

But it is not the case that the centralizing of education policy making in USED (in large part through re-authorizations of the 50 year-old Elementary and Secondary Education Act or ESEA) has so far visibly improved the education of low-achieving students or led to a closing of the gaps, however defined. In fact, centralization of education policy making in USED (currently via its approval of four-year State Plans) now seems to be damaging the purposes of all public educational institutions in this country. Policies or programs that were, to begin with, inappropriately designed for low achievers have been applied to the education of most higher-achieving students as well, regardless of race or ethnicity or national origin.

The end result is that most students (low and higher achievers) may be getting no better an education in the public schools than they have for years. Many may be getting a much worse education, to judge by (1) the number of students "opted" out of state-mandated tests in schools with large numbers of educated parents, and (2) a huge increase in homeschooling.

Moreover, it is no longer the case that education policy makers express concern if damage is done to all. Social goals have pre-empted educational goals, especially the development of rational thinking, in the name of self-esteem, "social justice" or "social and emotional learning." So, as many California educators (not parents) seem to have concluded, if all students can't handle Algebra I in grade 8, no one should be allowed to take it in grade 8 in a public school, or be required to take intermediate algebra in a community college.[10]

The entire public school system is being held hostage to the test scores of students many if not most of whom, for a range of reasons, are not academically inclined, do not attend school regularly, and/or do not like to read or write much. Other options need to be made available to them and/or their families. Good citizenship never depended on having a college education or a STEM career.

Chapters 1, 2, and 3 set forth the basic problems in education today and sketch the history and context of this country's efforts to address low achievement in its public schools, especially in the reading/English language arts curriculum. Chapter 4 explains how two major structural changes in the curriculum in the twentieth century, one at the high school level, the other in the middle grades, both designed to accommodate the lack of interest in reading in many low-achieving students, negatively impacted the reading and English curriculum for all students. Chapter 5 discusses a current description of the causes of low achievement in this country and reviews the major types of teaching strategies that have been used in the public schools to address them.

Chapter 6 addresses issues in defining and ensuring teacher quality. The focus is on teachers because they turned out to be the most important school-based factor in the 1966 Coleman Report, still considered a major reference for understanding the problems this country faces in achieving "equality of educational opportunity," the title of the report. While the major issue today is which trumps the other, teacher diversity or teacher quality, no one in a policy-making position suggests letting parents have a say about this.

Chapter 7 then addresses the testing concerns of both teachers and parents and suggests why short and frequent teacher-made tests might better address low achievers in this country than the excessive number of tests of endurance mandated by federal policy makers, and the many complaints about the amount of school instructional time spent on "teaching to the test." "Teaching to the test" is a relatively new term that describes efforts by schools to prepare students for tests mandated by a federal agency that wants to continue believing without evidence that test-based accountability for federal money improves low achievement.[11]

What Congress or state legislatures should beware of are attempts by so-called education policy makers to establish even worse policies than those they have already tried out, or, in desperation, to continue insisting that more funds be made available for failed or failing strategies. The rationale the public will be offered is that good intentions (their ideas) have not had sufficient support to be implemented well. Chapter 8 indicates some of the ideas that have been floated in attempts to make it seem that enacted education policies are working or to reinforce current policies.

Chapter 9 sums up what several education experts see as central issues to address in order to strengthen public education in this country for all students, keep students from dropping out of high school before graduation, and reduce low achievement. It also points out a few large-scale measures or programs that have raised the academic achievement or brightened the employment future of students who participated in them.

Chapter 10 concludes with several possible approaches to reducing massive adolescent underachievement and large numbers of high school drop-outs. Solutions are not possible when a country's educational institutions are still expected to solve a non-education-caused problem even though they haven't done so for over fifty years.

NOTES

1. David Figlio and Krzysztof Karbownik, "Some Schools Much Better Than Others at Closing Achievement Gaps Between Their Advantaged and Disadvantaged Students," *Education Next*, July 24, 2017, http://educationnext.org/some-schools-much-better-than-others-closing-achievement-gaps-between-their-advantaged-disadvantaged-students/.

2. Phillip Herman, Spencer Scanlan, Daisy Carreon, and McREL International. *Comparing enrollment, characteristics, and academic outcomes of students in developmental courses and those in credit-bearing courses at Northern Marianas College*, April 2017, https://files.eric.ed.gov/fulltext/ED573813.pdf.

3. Allie Bidwell, "American Students Fall in International Academic Tests, Chinese Lead the Pack," *U.S.News*, December 3, 2013, https://www.usnews.com/news/articles/2013/12/03/american-students-fall-in-international-academic-tests-chinese-lead-the-pack. About 25 percent did not reach "Level 2" on the 2012 PISA math test. See also "Characteristics of U.S.15-Year-Old Low Achievers in an International Context: Findings from PISA 2000," Statistical Analysis Report, *IES/NCES*, October 2005, http://files.eric.ed.gov/fulltext/ED488961.pdf.

4. "The Nation's Report Card 2015 Mathematics and Reading Assessments," https://www.nationsreportcard.gov/reading_math_2015/#reading/state/acl?grade=8.

5. "The Condition of Education," 2016, *IES/NCES*, http://files.eric.ed.gov/fulltext/ED565888.pdf, 88, or "Public School Enrollment, by Race/Ethnicity," Lucile Packard Foundation, June 2016.

6. Vanessa Wright, "More White Children in Low-Income Families than any other Racial Group," *National Center for Children in Poverty*, February 14, 2012, http://www.nccp.org/media/releases/release_138.html.

7. Linda Darling-Hammond, "Unequal Opportunity: Race and Education," *Brookings Institution*, March 1, 1998, https://www.brookings.edu/articles/unequal-opportunity-race-and-education/. "…educational outcomes for minority children are much more a function of their unequal access to key educational resources, including skilled teachers and quality curriculum…"

8. See as one example, Melinda Anderson, "How the Stress of Racism Affects Learning," *The Atlantic*, October 11, 2016, https://www.theatlantic.com/education/archive/2016/10/how-the-stress-of-racism-affects-learning/503567/.

9. For example, in relation to a 2015 report on the "black-white achievement gap," the National Center for Education Statistics (NCES) notes, on a page titled "black-white gaps FAQ," that "education policy can redistribute resources (as an example) such that even the portion of the gap attributable to SES differences is addressed," https://nces.ed.gov/nationsreportcard/studies/gaps/bwfaq.aspx.

10. Kyle Becker, "No, California, Requiring Students to Take Algebra Is Not a 'Civil Rights' Issue. Allowing Them to Skip It Is," *Independent Journal Review*, July 2017, http://ijr.com/the-declaration/2017/07/927625-no-california-requiring-students-take-algebra-not-civil-rights-issue-allowing-skip. See also Mikhail Zinshteyn, "Cal State drops intermediate algebra as requirement to take some college-level math courses," *EdSource*, August 1, 2017, https://edsource.org/2017/cal-state-drops-intermediate-algebra-requirement-allows-other-math-courses/585595.

11. For a more detailed description, see Sandra Stotsky, "Testing Limits," *Academic Questions*, 2016, 29, 285-98. http://web.a.ebscohost.com.proxy.library.vcu.edu/ehost/resultsadvanced.

ONE
The Current Education Problem

Ever since the end of World War II, this country has been seeking the holy grail in public education: reforms that would strengthen public education for all students and at the same time increase the academic achievement of large groups of low achievers. Until the mid-1960s, we seemed to be making some headway with the first part of the goal.

In 1956, the Council for Basic Education (CBE) was formed by prominent citizens to advocate for a strong liberal arts–oriented curriculum for all students,[1] in the spirit of the famed Committee of Ten's recommendations in 1892.[2] They had been aroused to action in large part by the description of public education as a "wasteland" in a best-selling book by historian Arthur Bestor in 1953.[3]

More sensational and influential than Bestor's book was Rudolph Flesch's *Why Johnny Can't Read*, in 1955,[4] a book highly critical of the brute memorization strategies taught to all prospective elementary teachers in our education schools as part of the "look, say" (sight word) method for beginning reading.

About the time that CBE was founded, the College Board began to develop Advanced Placement courses, not only to stimulate highly capable and motivated adolescents still in high school but also to reinvigorate those who would teach these courses.[5] The academic quality of our teaching force was of great concern at this time.

In the late 1950s, an authoritative study of the American high school by James B. Conant (president of Harvard University and a former chemistry professor) urged consolidation of our typically small public high schools, in large part to enable them to hire teachers who could offer the advanced coursework in mathematics and the sciences that academically oriented private schools (e.g., the famous New England boarding schools) gave students of wealthy parents.[6]

Consolidation had already begun in the late 1940s in many states, but Conant's book added urgency and impetus to the movement. Many small communities across the country formed regional high schools, overcoming small-town loyalties to their own athletic teams. They were then able to hire full-time high school mathematics and science teachers and strengthen high school mathematics and science curricula. Before consolidation, many small public high schools had no full-time high school math teachers or lab-oriented science teachers.

In part a response to Sputnik in 1957, Congress passed the National Defense Education Act (NDEA) in 1958, funding collaboration between academic experts at major universities across the country with experienced and talented K–12 teachers in the development of textbooks, course syllabi, and teacher institutes in all subjects and at all grade levels—all in the name of national defense.

Some Sputnik-era curricula had actually begun to be developed before Sputnik.[7] They all became part of an intellectually driven movement to reform the content and pedagogy of the entire school curriculum, largely under the leadership of Jerome Bruner of Harvard University and Jerrold Zacharias of MIT.[8]

When Admiral Hyman Rickover's *American Education: A National Failure* came out in 1963,[9] his complaints about the low standards for education in this country had long been in the news—and accepted as sound judgment by the broad public. James B. Conant's book on teacher education came out in 1963 as well—urging a complete rethinking and restructuring of teacher preparation.[10] This badly needed reform never began, although some of his many ideas have been implemented over the years.

Because they were erroneously perceived as aimed only at high achievers, and because many teachers found them difficult to teach, the Sputnik-era textbooks and course syllabi were heavily criticized by parents and then abandoned by the schools. In a book on the "standards" wars in the states and nationally, published in 2000, Ralph Raimi and Mary Campbell Gallagher provide analytical accounts of what happened to the curriculum and pedagogical reforms of the Sputnik era from their perspective as two of the academic participants (in mathematics and English respectively).[11]

BEGINNING OF DIRECT FEDERAL INVOLVEMENT IN LOCAL PUBLIC EDUCATION

Public attention turned in the blink of an eye to a heavily funded piece of legislation by Congress in 1965 (Elementary and Secondary Education Act or ESEA), designed to improve directly the education of low-achieving African Americans and children on tribal reservations. ESEA was part of President Lyndon B. Johnson's War on Poverty.

It is still difficult over a half century later to understand why the need to strengthen public education for all students was shunted aside so rapidly—and so completely. The sharp decline in SAT Verbal and Mathematics scores in the early 1960s should have made it clear that public education as a whole needed to be made stronger if possible in a country that wanted more not fewer students in college.[12] But the idea of strengthening all of public education was almost completely abandoned as the need to improve the education of low-performing students came to consume public attention. It is not clear why so few seemed to think that the second goal could be achieved as part of strengthening the public school system for all students—a goal that was turned on its head fifty years later, despite a sharp decline in high performance on the SAT in the 1970s and 1980s that has never been reversed.[13]

ESEA's purpose in 1965 was in fact to "strengthen public education" as well as to improve "educational opportunities" for low-achieving students by targeting extra funds for their schools and teachers. Congress knew that public education in general was not in good condition—it had heard what Admiral Rickover had been saying for over a decade.

Nevertheless, the distribution of ESEA's funds centered on the relatively small proportion of students then who needed special attention, and little or no attention was paid to the needs of the vast majority of students in the public schools. Worse yet, Congress did not understand that educators themselves did not know how to increase the academic achievement of large numbers of very low-achieving students.[14]

Many had ideas (i.e., theories) but little to show their actual effectiveness (i.e., empirical data). A ceaseless flow of federal and private funds enabled an army of education entrepreneurs to try out their ideas without consequences for any of them and without demands for change in teacher recruitment for and preparation in our education schools.

Education schools were reluctant, then as now, to teach effective approaches to beginning reading or to call for the testing of content knowledge in licensure tests of prospective teachers of young students. Despite the accumulating research evidence against a "meaning" approach (versus a "decoding" approach) in beginning reading, many if not most education school faculty continued their emphasis on guessing and memorization (also called Whole Language and, later, Balanced Literacy).

Many publishers were willing to address Flesch's criticisms and experiment with teaching wherever possible words exhibiting consistent relationships between symbols and sounds in basal readers, the instructional reading materials for the primary grades. (The well-known Merrill Readers were one perhaps extreme example.) But education school faculty had a firm grip on teacher preparation and were not about to give up easily their monopoly on what was taught in the public school classroom and how. Education schools had earlier ensured that an attempt at national teacher licensure tests—the National Teacher Examinations—focused more on pedagogy than content.[15]

Nor was it easy to loosen education schools' grip on policies flowing from a state's own department of education (or public instruction), whose staff had been mostly trained in education schools. It wasn't until the early 1990s that Massachusetts was able to pass a comprehensive Education Reform Act requiring accountability from its education schools—in the form, chiefly, of candidates for a teaching license having to pass both skills-oriented and subject matter licensure tests.

The state was successful by the early 1990s in reforming public education mainly because of massive support from the business community, which had become annoyed at footing the bills to educate on their own premises semi-literate high school graduates. Teacher and administrator preparation for K–12 had always been a state or local function and had long reflected a strong dose of Rousseau. Education school–based educators were also and have continued to be among the chief consultants to publishers. It would never be easy in any state to reduce the influence of education schools on the public school curriculum. The help the business community gave the Massachusetts legislature made a huge difference.

Even though there's been little evidence since 1965 that federal funds have increased the academic achievement of low achievers by high school, especially reading skills, Congress has continuously increased funding for Title I and other programs targeting low achievers in its various reauthorizations of ESEA. Even if Congress felt it had no choice but to pony up the money for the education of low achievers, why did it believe local educators knew how to spend the appropriated money effectively? We do not know.

Or did it not matter how federal money was spent so long as Congress could show that money was appropriated? Federal funding, as well as Whole Language and its counterpart in arithmetic in the primary grades ("reform math"), were all turned into civil rights issues for Hispanics as well as African Americans and children in tribal reservation schools despite the failure of ESEA reauthorizations to advance significantly their academic achievement on reading and mathematics tests sponsored by the National Assessment of Educational Progress (NAEP) or on other indices of achievement.

And this despite the fact that just about every imaginable program or strategy has been tried out in our public schools. Moreover, policy makers and educators have tried out ideas and strategies that were or became philosophically and pedagogically exact opposites of each other. As one example of a set of contradictory "reforms," consider what happened to "remediation," the first major concept to dominate "reform." Early efforts to boost low achievers aimed to give them focused teaching time *within* the school day.

This philosophy was embedded in remedial classes stimulated by the original 1965 ESEA. Schools provided remedial classes for reading and arithmetic in the elementary grades, with trained teachers in charge of these typically small classes. At the high school level, remediation was provided by courses in the lowest curriculum track or tutors. In public colleges, low-achieving students who were admitted were assessed and placed into remedial or non-credit classes, most often in reading or mathematics. The assumption behind remediation was that something needed to be restored or brought back up to a norm—and could be.

In contrast to remediating low achievers *within* the school day, other policy makers and educators believed that low achievers needed more time to learn *beyond the school day*, to compensate for being slower learners. This assumption underlay special summer school programs or after-school remedial programs and, in recent years, longer school days.

However, no body of research has yet shown a marked increase in academic performance after low achievers had been given focused remediation during the school day or additional time on task beyond the school day and outside the usual academic calendar. Nor have remedial classes for college freshmen enabled the majority of students completing them to go on to complete a four-year college degree program. Remediation has become a synonym for a long-term failed strategy whether within or beyond the usual academic day or calendar.

As another example of a set of contradictory "reforms," consider the efforts to alter the academic status of low achievers in the name of boosting self-esteem. Some strategies or programs were designed to give low-achieving students much more to learn, academically speaking, than what was offered in remedial classes and to remove the epithet of slow learner. These changes were based on the assumption that placement in a remedial class sapped the motivation or self-esteem of low-achieving students or that low-achieving students were being deprived of the knowledge and skills taught to high-achieving children when they were placed in remedial classes or in homogeneous classes for low achievers. The separation of students into more homogeneous achievement-based classes had been considered a reform in junior high schools when it was introduced by "progressive" educators at the beginning of the twentieth century.[16]

Later, instead of separate remedial classes in the elementary grades, one could find "pull-outs" or in-class aides working side by side with the classroom teacher in self-contained classes, or an expensive tutorial program called Reading Recovery in the primary grades but without demonstrable long-term results to justify its costs.[17] The "basic" track in high schools (the bottom level for major courses) disappeared, but the huge spread in reading skills as cohorts of students moved up the grades remained. High school graduation rates increased, as did enrollment in state and community colleges. The remedial course at the college level was usually called a developmental or basic course—but it was still without academic credit because it taught mainly high school–level content or less. The extent to which higher enrollment in college has led to an increase in remedial courses is disputed.[18] It also became popular to encourage open enrollment for advanced placement (AP) classes in high school whether or not an interested student had the requisite academic background.[19]

New concepts were developed to camouflage low achievement in African Americans in particular (because they comprised the most easily identifiable group of low achievers at the time) or to motivate them based on an assumption that they were alienated by a curriculum developed for non-black students. Black low achievers were not to be viewed as having "language" deficits or differences. Instead, attempts were made to give status to their use of an oral dialect with grammatical differences from Standard English by the development of dialect-based instructional reading materials (an unsuccessful project mainly because black teachers and parents rejected them) and, later, by dignifying their dialect with a name, "Ebonics."

"Afro-centric" curricula were proposed on the grounds that studying their own history and literary writers would motivate African American students academically. Multiculturalism swept aside study of the main currents in U.S. history and literature on the grounds that the cultures of all identifiable groups, here and elsewhere, were inherently equal and worthy of study (whether or not they contributed significantly to the evolution of the English language—the language of instruction in most secondary and postsecondary institutions of education in this country.

Although these movements altered the school curriculum for many students quite dramatically, none moved the needle on the academic status of African Americans as a group. As a group, they remained on the bottom floor of the academic skyscraper, with Hispanics (as they first came to be called as their numbers increased in the latter half of the twentieth century to the point where they became identifiable as a group) not much higher than them, but with Asian Americans moving rapidly to the top floors ahead of "whites."

"Accelerated schools" for low-achieving students in urban areas were another popular approach.[20] So far, the idea has not borne much fruit. According to a careful evaluation, high expectations and high academic status for low achievers in accelerated schools have not resulted uniformly in such major long-term benefits as higher high school graduation rates and greater credit accumulation, compared to their peers in non-accelerated schools.[21]

> [T]he findings on graduation and credit accumulation indicate that accelerated schools have benefited the academic outcomes of both earlier and more recent entrants into their programs. . . . [However, a] strict

interpretation of this evidence would conclude only that certain providers have more beneficial impacts on their particular sets of enrollees than other providers do on their particular sets of enrollees (29).

By the mid-1990s, remediation as the major strategy for addressing low achievement was being replaced by an extensive regimen of testing for the purpose of accountability—a new concept in education, meaning that educators (not the students themselves) were to be held responsible for student achievement. At first—under the 2001 reauthorization of ESEA called No Child Left Behind (NCLB)—schools (in effect, their administrators) were held accountable; later, in 2010, the Race to the Top (RttT) grant competition sought to make teachers responsible.

The first inkling of testing as a strategy to upgrade low achievers' academic performance came in the Clinton administration. In 1997, President Clinton proposed developing a National Voluntary Reading Test in grade four and a National Voluntary Mathematics Test in grade eight.[22] Development of both tests, however, was killed by Congress in 1998.

Nevertheless, in the 2001 reauthorization of ESEA, under President George W. Bush, test-based accountability became the primary strategy for addressing low achievement, based on several questionable assumptions: (1) Teachers and/or administrators are responsible for low achievement. (2) They don't have high enough expectations for low achievers. (3) They don't know how to identify low achievers without constant testing. (4) Tests motivate low achievers to do better even if the scores have no consequences for them. The strategy had seemed to work in Texas but didn't transfer well to the national level. Bottom line: Reform of the school curriculum and teacher education toward the goal that all students needed to improve academically was dead.

Despite the growing backlash to excessive (and useless) national testing, which was expanded under President Obama in the 2015 reauthorization of ESEA, this country is now experiencing another transition in how to address low achievement. In contrast to attempts to elevate the academic status of low achievers by accelerating their learning pace in "accelerated schools" or by allowing them to enroll in Advanced Placement (AP) courses without the usual pre-admission level of achievement (or in other ways), "reformers" have sought since 2010 to give them less to learn by focusing on skills or competencies, not academic knowledge. Common Core's English language arts standards, the tests based on them, and the drive for competency-based teaching and testing are current examples.

Development of workforce-related skills has become the umbrella for efforts to reduce the academic content of every subject in the curriculum. Reductions in content taught have so far been achieved by the establishment of minimal content standards and tests based on them for the Next Generation Science Standards and for new social studies standards (where they have been developed since 2015 or so), and by the inclusion of content-empty standards for social and emotional learning (SEL) in every academic subject and in many state accountability plans, despite the lack of a sound body of classroom-based evidence attesting to SEL's usefulness and a classroom teacher's ability to address such standards.[23]

CONCLUDING REMARKS

Assumptions about the causes of and solutions to low achievement have changed dramatically. But nothing has worked—to judge by the (long-term trend tests NAEP began as the Nation's Report Cards around 1970)—to increase academic achievement in large groups of low achievers. Attempts to equalize what is taught in a state by the use of state or national standards have not altered differences in what is learned—that is, the "gaps" have so far not disappeared between "overachieving" and underachieving groups by grade twelve. The 2015 NAEP scores show a decline or stagnation in grades four and eight as full implementation of Common Core's standards took place for the Common Core–based state tests given in 2014/5."[24] Elimination of homogeneous (achievement-based) classes (in reading and mathematics) in urban middle schools have not led to higher grade eight scores on NAEP tests for low achievers, and arguments for reintroducing homogeneous classes in urban areas (to provide a challenge to able minority youngsters) are now being made.[25]

Nor have the reading levels of college textbooks changed. They still require at the least high school–level reading skills. This country has moved from a medical model (remediation) to a test-based accountability model, and is now in transition to a workforce development model[26] dominated by skills teaching and testing to address low achievement among African Americans and Hispanics.[27] But the workforce development model, unlike the remediation model, encompasses the entire public school system, P–20, or from preschool to postsecondary education, and all of the students in it.

Instead of strengthening the curriculum for all students, educators and education researchers seem to be aiming for a proletarian education for all—sufficient literacy and numeracy skills for many employers' workforce needs. Instead of aiming for a strong liberal arts curriculum for all public school students in K–12, preparing them for independent thinking, the goal now seems to be a K–12 curriculum that trains all students for the workforce.[28]

Education policy leaders also seem to be repudiating the reforms of the curriculum and pedagogy begun after World War II and ignoring the reason for these reforms—that is, declining academic standards for most students before, during, or after the war, whether in the name of "life adjustment," "real-world" education, or another non-academic goal. It is increasingly less tenable that low achievement as a widespread group phenomenon in middle and high school can be addressed quickly if at all by educational institutions without changing drastically all the educational and civic goals of all educational institutions. The pretense continues, however, as self-appointed policy makers refuse to learn from research and/or the past.

KEY IDEAS TO REMEMBER

1. After World War II, prominent citizens became alarmed at the low quality of public education, judging to some extent by what the military had found lacking during the war.
2. In 1957, Sputnik shocked the nation and stimulated Congress to pass the National Defense in Education Act (NDEA) in 1958.
3. The NDEA helped to spark and support a vast Curriculum Reform movement led by prominent academics collaborating with talented K–12 teachers to develop new textbooks, lessons, and training institutes for K–12 in all subjects and at all grade levels. The movement lasted for less than a decade.
4. In 1965, Congress passed ESEA as part of President Johnson's War on Poverty, switching attention suddenly to low achievers even though educators didn't know how to reduce massive low achievemnt in adolescence.
5. Despite a range of efforts to reduce low achievement in the groups ESEA had been intended for, these groups made little academic progress. ESEA was always re-authorized by Congress and with increasing appropriations.
6. ESEA now seeks to close "achievement gaps" among unspecified groups.
7. Education policy makers seem to be repudiating the kinds of K–12 curriculum and teacher education reforms that experts began or talked about after World War II.
8. Many education policy makers want the public schools to adopt mental health or socio-emotional standards (SEL), without ensuring that teachers or tests assessing socio-emotional learning are supervised by a child psychiatrist or clinical psychologist.

NOTES

1. Council for Basic Education—History, Activities, Governance Legal Status and Publications, Assessment of CBE's Influence and Significance, http://education.stateuniversity.com/pages/1888/Council-Basic-Education.html. CBE closed down in 2004, http://www.edweek.org/ew/articles/2004/07/14/42cbe.h23.html.

2. "Council for Basic Education—History, Activities, Governance Legal Status and Publications, Assessment of CBE's Influence and Significance," State University, http://education.stateuniversity.com/pages/1888/Council-Basic-Education.html. See Wikipedia for a description of the Committee of Ten's recommendations: https://en.wikipedia.org/wiki/Committee_of_Ten. CBE closed its doors in 2004: David J. Hoff, "Council for Basic Education Closes Its Door," *Education Week*, July 14, 2004, http://www.edweek.org/ew/articles/2004/07/14/42cbe.h23.html.

3. Arthur Bestor, *Educational Wastelands: The Retreat from Learning in Our Public Schools* (Urbana-Champaign: University of Illinois Press, 1953).

4. Rudolf Flesch, *Why Johnny Can't Read and What You Can Do About It* (New York: Harper & Row Publishers, 1955), https://www.goodreads.com/book/show/821826.Why_Johnny_Can_t_Read_And_What_You_Can_Do_About_It.

5. College Board, "Advance Placement Program," http://www.collegeboard.com/prod_downloads/about/news_info/ap/ap_history_english.pdf.

6. James B. Conant, *The American High School Today* (New York: McGraw-Hill, 1959).

7. Many of the scholars and programs involved are noted in Rodger W. Bybee, "The Sputnik Era: Why Is This Educational Reform Different from All Other Reforms?," http://scholar.google.com/scholar_url?url=http://www.nas.edu/sputnik/bybee.doc&hl=en&sa=X&scisig=AAGBfm1eyyr4v4a45_hHvUbFiPt1cjs3Yw&nossl=1&oi=scholarr.

8. Peter Dow, "Reflecting on Sputnik: Linking the Past, Present, and Future of Educational Reform," National Academy of Sciences, http://www.nas.edu/sputnik/dow2.htm

9. "Hyman Rickover," *Wikipedia*, https://en.wikipedia.org/wiki/Hyman_G._Rickover#Focus_on_education.

10. James B. Conant, *The Education of American Teachers* (New York: McGraw-Hill, 1963).

11. Ralph Raimi, "Judging State Standards for K–12 Mathematics Education," and Mary Campbell Gallagher, "Lessons from the Sputnik-Era Curriculum Reform Movement," in *What's at Stake in the K–12 Standards Wars*, ed. Sandra Stotsky (New York: Peter Lang, 2000).

12. David G. Savage, "The Long Decline in SAT Scores," *Educational Leadership*, January 1978, http://www.ascd.org/ASCD/pdf/journals/ed_lead/el_197801_savage.pdf.

13. According to education policy consultant David Barulich, "In 1972 over 116,000 students scored above 600 on the verbal S.A.T. In 1982 fewer than 71,000 scored that high even though a similar number took the exam." (Quoted by M. D. Aeschliman in a review of E. D. Hirsch's book *Why Knowledge Matters* in the *National Review*, February 18, 2017, http://www.nationalreview.com/article/445038/educational-reformer-hirsch-promotes-knowledge-against-its-enemies).

14. Emma Brown, "What Should America Do about Its Worst Public Schools? States Still Don't Seem to Know," *Washington Post*, August 6, 2017, https://www.washingtonpost.com/local/education/what-should-america-do-about-its-worst-public-schools-states-still-dont-seem-to-know/2017/08/06/db2d6dcc-76c6-11e7-8839-ec48ec4cae25_story.html?utm_term=.4c25c811e48d&wpisrc=nl_sb_smartbrief.

15. See chapter 4 in Sandra Stotsky, *An Empty Curriculum: The Need to Reform Teacher Licensing Regulations and Tests* (Lanham, MD: Rowman & Littlefield, 2015).

16. "Academic Tracking in the Schools," http://ga-academictracking.weebly.com/history-of-academic-tracking.html.

17. Pamela Cook, Deborah R. Rodes, and Kay L. Lipsitz, "The Reading Wars and Reading Recovery: What Educators, Families, and Taxpayers Should Know," *Journal of Learning Disabilities* 22, no. 2 (August 2017), http://js.sagamorepub.com/ldmj/article/view/8391/6079.

18. The remediation rate for college freshmen seems to be between 20 and 40 percent. Laura Jimenez, Scott Sargrad, Jessica Morales, and Maggie Thompson, "Remedi-

al Education: The Cost of Catching Up, Center for American Progress," September 28, 2016, https://www.americanprogress.org/issues/education/reports/2016/09/28/144000/remedial-education/; and Valerie Strauss, "How College Remediation Rates Are Distorted and Why," *Washington Post*, July 7, 2014, https://www.washingtonpost.com/news/answer-sheet/wp/2014/07/07/how-college-remediation-rates-are-distorted-and-why/?utm_term=.7d7bea308ca9. However, most students taking remedial courses do not complete a college degree program, although the percentage is not clear. AACC, "About Completion Challenge," http://www.aacc.nche.edu/About/completionchallenge/Documents/Completion-Fact_Sheet.pdf.

19. Stephanie Simon, "AP Classes Failing Students," *Politico*, August 21, 2013, http://www.politico.com/story/2013/08/education-advanced-placement-classes-tests-095723.

20. Howard Bloom, Sandra Ham, Laura Melton, and Julieanne O'Brien, "Evaluating the Accelerated Schools Approach: A Look at Early Implementation and Impacts on Student Achievements in Eight Elementary Schools," *Building Knowledge to Improve Social Policy*, November 2001, accessed January 30, 2018, http://www.mdrc.org/publication/evaluating-accelerated-schools-approach.

21. Hanley Chiang and Brian Gill, The Impacts of Philadelphia's Accelerated Schools on Academic Progress and Graduation, Final Report, November 23, 2010, accessed January 30, 2018, http://www.projectuturn.net/docs/impacts.pdf.

22. "Clinto Proposes National Exam, Again," n.d., accessed January 30, 2018, http://fairtest.org/clinton-proposes-national-exam-again; and http://library.cqpress.com/cqresearcher/document.php?id=cqresrre1999051400.

23. Jane Robbins, "Schools Ditch Academics for Emotional Manipulation," *The National Pulse* (read the full article at *The Federalist*), October 19, 2016, accessed January 30, 2018, https://thenationalpulse.com/commentary/schools-ditch-academics-for-emotional-manipulation/.

24. See Valerie Strauss, "What the New NAEP Scores Really Tell Us," *Answer Sheet*, May 3, 2016, accessed January 29, 2018, https://www.washingtonpost.com/news/answer-sheet/wp/2016/05/03/what-the-new-naep-test-scores-really-tell-us/?utm_term=.8bbb0a0d6a3a; and Eric Lerum, "The New NAEP Results and What They Tell Us," *Education Post*, October 28, 2015, accessed January 30, 2018, http://educationpost.org/the-new-naep-results-and-what-they-tell-us/. But see Fordham Institute's blog on a few rays of hope since the 1990s: Kate Walsh, "Silent Progress on Education," *Flypaper*, August 11, 2017, accessed January 30, 2018, https://edexcellence.net/articles/silent-progress-on-education.

25. Liz Sablich, "Helping to Level the AP Playing Field: Why Eighth Grade math Matters More Than You Think," *Brown Center Chalkboard*, April 4, 2016, accessed January 30, 2018, https://www.brookings.edu/blog/brown-center-chalkboard/2016/04/04/helping-to-level-the-ap-playing-field-why-eighth-grade-math-matters-more-than-you-think/.

26. "Strategies for K–12 and Workforce Alignment," *Achieve*, June 2010, https://www.achieve.org/files/StrategiesforK-12andWorkforceAlignment.pdf.

27. "Strategies for K–12 and Workforce Alignment," *Achieve*, June 2010, accessed January 30, 2018, https://www.achieve.org/files/StrategiesforK-12andWorkforceAlignment.pdf.

28. Congressional Hearings on Education and the Workforce for 2017, accessed January 30, 2018, https://edworkforce.house.gov/calendar/list.aspx?EventTypeID=189.

TWO
The Current Political Context for the Education of Low-Achieving Students

Federalism refers to a balance of power between a central government and the various states or provinces in a country, each component of government having powers and responsibilities of its own. Even though we have three levels of government in the United States—federal, state, and local, each with the power to tax and to make laws of its own—federalism in this country refers not to a balance between the federal government and local units (or local and state units) but only to a balance between the federal government and state governments. Constitutionally, local government is under state government.

Thus, an increase in state control of something may mean a decrease in local control—whether or not federal control has seemingly decreased. And local taxpayers seem to have little control of that "something"—their own public schools—under the Every Student Succeeds Act (ESSA), the 2015 reauthorization of the Elementary and Secondary Education Act (ESEA), first authorized in 1965 as part of President Lyndon B. Johnson's "War on Poverty."[1]

EVERY STUDENT SUCCEEDS ACT OF DECEMBER 2015

Remarkably, the claim by Every Student Succeeds Act advocates such as Senator Lamar Alexander of Tennessee—that it restores (some) authority to both state and local governments at the same time it reduces federal control of local schools—has not been recognized as the fraudulent claim it is. ESSA has neither increased local control of any policies governing a local district's public schools nor increased the authority of a governor or state legislature.

Instead, ESSA has elevated the role of staff in state departments of education (which is mainly appointed) and, to a lesser extent, the (mostly appointed) boards of education typically in charge of them, the members of which tend to follow the directives they have been given if they want to keep their seats. State board members are usually not paid for the little they actually do; their main purpose today is not to ask questions but to approve the policies desired by the U.S. Department of Education. (That was the case under Arne Duncan and John King Jr., the education secretaries appointed by President Barack Obama, and it's the case now under Trump appointee Betsy DeVos, who oversees many Duncan and King appointees embedded in the department.)

That's true even when federal education policies have demonstrably failed to produce "equal outcomes" across different student groups and seem, instead, to be widening the "gaps." Equal outcomes, moreover, were not the goal of the Elementary and Secondary Education Act in 1965, even though closing "gaps" is the explicit goal today of the 2015 reauthorization of ESEA, known as the Every Student Succeeds Act.

The Elementary and Secondary Education Act of fifty-two years ago was the first major attempt by the federal government to improve the education of low-achieving children—at the time (1965) mainly black children and children on tribal reservations in the West or elsewhere. Its goal was to give them an opportunity to take advantage of a stronger public education system than the one that was serving other children in the post-World War II years. ESEA's stated purpose in 1965 was to "strengthen and improve educational quality and educational opportunities in the Nation's elementary and secondary schools." It seemed to imply that Congress intended to strengthen all children's education.

However, the appropriating of federal money, with or without strings attached, to improve the education of low-achieving children or their schools has not been effective, to judge by the nation's so-called "Report Cards" (officially known as National Assessment of Educational Progress, or NAEP tests) since the 1970s. Education researchers have also acknowledged the failure of test-based accountability in particular, as it was conceptualized in the 2001 re-authorization of ESEA known as No Child Left Behind. As economist and education researcher Helen Ladd commented on a 2010 Brookings Institution paper by Thomas Dee and Brian Jacob:

> First, the null findings for reading indicate to me that to the extent that higher reading scores are an important goal for this country, NCLB is clearly not the right approach. That raises the obvious follow-up question: What is? The suggestive evidence that I have included here on Massachusetts [indicates] that states may be in a better position to promote student achievement than the federal government.

As a substitute for test-based accountability, Ladd also proposed school inspections—a practice in many other countries.[2]

Despite the lack of empirical evidence that an infusion of federal money into state and urban school budgets improved the education of or schools attended by low-achieving children, ESEA has been reauthorized over the years, with increased appropriations in each successive version. Puzzlingly, lack of research evidence has not stimulated rigorous research (funded by the federal government or the nation's many foundations, for example) into why so little if any progress occurred in fifty years and how federal money has actually been used by the public schools or departments of education that spent it. Nor has lack of evidence of positive results from allocating more money for the education of low-achieving children reduced the range of compensatory or supplementary programs funded by the U.S. Department of Education for them or for teachers in the form of professional development.

Au contraire, it has led education policy makers to come up with ever-more-costly and damaging changes in educational practices in their attempt to solve what may be ultimately a non-educational problem—a problem that cannot be solved by the schools no matter how much money Congress or state legislatures vote to give local school districts in the name of equity or compensation for the low-achieving students they happen to enroll. Lack of positive results also led education policy makers to transform the purpose of the Elementary and Secondary Education Act in its 2015 reauthorization from educational to social.

CHANGES IN THE PURPOSE OF THE ELEMENTARY AND SECONDARY EDUCATION ACT

Transforming a reasonable educational goal (that is, strengthening education for all) into a non-educational problem can be seen in the subtle but meaningful change in the purpose of the Elementary and Secondary Education Act in its 2015 reauthorization (Every Student Succeeds Act, or ESSA). Its purposes are now "to provide all children significant opportunity to receive a fair, equitable, and high-quality education, and to close educational achievement gaps."[3] It is unclear why no one has criticized ESSA on the grounds that its unknown writers had changed the basic purpose of the original legislation in two key respects. ESEA was now aimed at providing fairness and equality in educational opportunity for "all" children and at closing "achievement gaps."

The goal was no longer strengthening the education of all children or even all disadvantaged children. Nor did the Every Student Succeeds Act identify the groups with "gaps" between them. (To this day, we don't know who wrote and paid for the thousand-plus-page bill that ESSA is.)

HOW TO ADDRESS UNDEFINED EQUAL OUTCOMES NOT CAUSED BY THE EDUCATION SYSTEM?

It is clear to education school faculties that our education system (and perhaps education professors' role in its effectiveness) is not the cause of low academic achievement. As a faculty member of an education school acknowledged in a 2014 paper she and her graduate students gave at a civil rights conference, "differences in achievement across different student populations represent influences beyond the purview of the education system."[4] The author recommends that we "expand" the definition of equity in the policies and resources made available to the schools and other institutions, presumably until "equal outcomes" are achieved, although she doesn't tell us exactly what that phrase means and when we might return to a non-expansive definition of equity.

What she and others of her persuasion (and they are legion) don't tell us is what exactly the schools or other institutions should spend more money on or what policies we should put into place (in the name of expanding the definition of equity) that would lead to equal outcomes. After over fifty years of ESEA, and billions on education research, we still don't know.

Nor is it clear that a paucity of empirical clues matters. Apparently, this researcher and her colleagues across the country want to achieve "equal outcomes" across different student populations, whether or not there is evidence to support their ideas on a small scale, never mind a large scale. The only thing they seem to agree on is spending more money on a possibly unobtainable goal that local taxpayers have not voted on and instituting unspecified policies to try to achieve it. Nor can we find a discussion of why the United States or any country should aim for "equal outcomes" across politically defined student groups. Indeed, the educational goal was once closer to self-actualization for individuals, not proportional similarities for groups. High and low achievers alike worked out their own occupational destinies.

KEY IDEAS TO REMEMBER

1. The publicly unknown authors of the 2015 re-authorization of ESEA, called Every Student Shall Succeed (ESSA), made closing "achievement gaps" the chief purpose of the ESEA, not strengthening public education.
2. ESSA did not identify the groups with gaps between them that were to be closed, or explain how the gaps were to be determined. To this day, it is not public knowledge who wrote and paid for the over-1,000-page ESSA.

3. At a civil rights conference, an education school professor asserted that "differences in achievement across different student populations represent influences beyond the purview of the education system."
4. Education schools have offered no ideas on what these influences are or suggestions on how to achieve "equal outcomes" within or beyond "the purview of the education system."
5. No discussion of the meaning of "equal outcomes" in education can be found in the professional literature in education or political science.

NOTES

1. https://www.gpo.gov/fdsys/pkg/STATUTE-79-Pg27.pdf.
2. Helen F. Ladd, "Now Is the Time to Experiment with Inspections for School Accountability," *Brookings Institution*, May 26, 2016.
3. https://legcousel.house.gov/Comps/Elementary%20And%20Secondary%20Education%20Act%20Of%201965.pdf, 9.
4. Andy Elder, "Promise of Equality from Common Core Not So Easily Achieved," Penn State School of Education, December 2014, https://ed.psu.edu/news/news-oct-dec-2014/kornhaber.

THREE
Early U.S. Educational History

This chapter notes major highlights in American education until mid-twentieth century. Of importance were those affecting the general curriculum for low achievers and/or those students not intending to go on to college.

It is well known that early New England Puritans expected all Puritan communities to provide a primary education for their children so that, as Protestants, they could read the Bible themselves. At first, their focus was on boys (Boston Latin School, founded in 1635, was free but for boys only; Harvard College was founded in 1636—also for boys—chiefly for the training of ministers and lawyers).

By the eighteenth century, both girls and boys attended the grammar school each town was obliged to provide in exchange for permission to incorporate as a town. Because school attendance was not compulsory, students could leave at any age for work on the family farm, in the home, or for an apprenticeship.

It was relatively simple to ensure the primary education of children who didn't like going to school, reading, writing, or doing arithmetic. Just teach them, grade by grade, whatever was taught to their age peers, and whatever they were willing to do in school until they left school—often in the upper elementary grades and before graduation from a grade eight "grammar" school. So long as they weren't idle or getting into mischief regularly like a Tom Sawyer, no one much minded school-leavers.

For centuries, apprenticeships were common ways for young adolescents to learn a trade in Europe and America. Those who were sufficiently interested or willing to study, read, write, and do arithmetic (or wanted to become ministers or lawyers) continued on after graduation from grade eight in a grammar school to a publicly or privately funded high school education. At the turn of the twentieth century, only about 3–5 percent of the school-age population, more girls than boys, went to high school.[1]

PRE–WORLD WAR II K–12 EDUCATION

The Industrial Revolution was a major driver of child labor outside the home, leading many low- and high-achieving children into the workforce. During the late eighteenth and early nineteenth centuries, Great Britain became the first country to industrialize. Because of this, it was also the first country where the nature of children's work changed so dramatically that child labor became seen as a social problem and a political issue.[2] Public concern mounted about young children who left school to work in factories or mines because their families needed whatever they could earn.

The regulation of child labor began in the earliest days of the Industrial revolution. The first act to regulate child labor in Britain was passed in 1803. As early as 1802 and 1819 Factory Acts were passed to confine the working hours of workhouse children in factories and cotton mills to twelve hours per day. However, the number of children working in factories eventually declined—for reasons that are still not clear.

There are many opinions regarding the reason(s) for the diminished role of child labor in these industries. Social historians believe it was the rise of the domestic ideology of the father as breadwinner and the mother as housewife that was embedded in the upper and middle classes and spread to the working-class. Economic historians argue it was the rise in the standard of living that accompanied the Industrial Revolution that allowed parents to keep their children home.[3]

Other scholars argued that the reduction of child labor came about because families started showing an interest in education and began sending their children to school voluntarily. Mandatory schooling laws in Great Britain came late and therefore did *not* play a role in the reduction of child labor as they may have done in the United States.

DEVELOPMENT OF THE "COMPREHENSIVE" HIGH SCHOOL

In this country, secondary schooling was accessible to those who wanted to attend high school. Despite the academic myth that American public high schools in the nineteenth century served only a college-intending population, they were already very flexible institutions by 1900, as Isaac Kandel characterized them.[4] In large part, this was because a grade eight graduation from a "grammar" school often meant the student had reached a college or adult reading level (by today's standards).[5]

The ideal of one high school for all children in the community appealed to most Americans, despite the option of private schools for the children of wealthy or religious parents. But there were very practical reasons why the curriculum in a town's high school had to be flexible; most of its students did not graduate or go on to college.

American public high schools in the latter half of the nineteenth century usually had a college preparatory program, especially if there was no nearby private academy to which a town might send academically promising students (and tuition payments). But very few students attended a public high school at the time,[6] even fewer graduated from a public high school, and very few of those who did graduate from a public or private school went to college.[7]

It is not widely known that most public high schools in the nineteenth century served many students who did not intend to go to college even if they did complete high school. In 1899–1900, there were about sixty-two thousand high school graduates of an estimated five hundred nineteen thousand students enrolled in grades nine through twelve, with an average of ninety-nine days attended per pupil, ages five to seventeen.[8]

The passage of compulsory school attendance laws in state after state, beginning in Massachusetts in 1852, may have caused many students to stay on in school at least through the first or second high school grade. By 1900, thirty states required school attendance until age fourteen, which covered grade eight but might mean grade nine or ten for many students.[9] By 1918, all states had such laws. From their early inception (and to this day) the laws across states varied. Laws specified the age at which a child had to enter school, and the age at which a child could obtain a work permit. They varied greatly across states in both their specifications and enforcement. According to one researcher, "These laws affected white men and women equally but had no effect on blacks. They were more effective in the southern and northern states than in the rest of the country."[10]

To address non-college-intending students' interests, small public high schools in the nineteenth century offered many courses in a variety of subjects to small numbers of students. To this day, some small Arkansas high schools offer almost as many courses as the number of students in them.[11] This range of courses satisfied local communities, which until well after World War II were completely financially responsible for their public schools.

In addition to catering to a large range of student needs, most if not all communities had traditionally supported an egalitarian thrust for the high school—that is, all students would attend the same high school despite differences in family income or intended careers—making the comprehensive high school that most students attended a "uniquely-American invention."[12] The down side was that in public high schools with fewer than one hundred students (true of over half of our public high schools in 1900), only 50 percent of the teachers were college graduates, limiting the range and rigor of what was taught in academic courses.[13]

In contrast, as one might expect, teachers in large urban high schools were apt to be far more academically qualified than their rural colleagues. Moreover, non-college-intending students in large urban high schools could usually enroll in a sequence of non-college preparatory courses as part of a commercial or vocational program, an enticement to complete high school. While the teaching force and curriculum in urban schools were usually superior to those in non-urban schools, there were serious limitations to the teachers and the curriculum in urban schools.

AWARENESS OF HIGH SCHOOL WEAKNESSES

In his brief comments on the history of K–12 mathematics, mathematician Ralph Raimi noted,

> With the great changes due to immigration and technologically driven increases in standard of living in the new [twentieth] century, however . . . the earlier grades had to take account of a possible high school future for their grade 8 graduates. For mathematics, this presented a special problem, since its more advanced levels—algebra, geometry, and trigonometry, were not the stuff of daily life; nor was the average product of a normal school (as teachers colleges were once styled) equipped to teach it.[14]

The U.S. Army's needs in World War II turned out to be a wake-up call. Public education everywhere was in need of upgrading, especially in mathematics and science. As Ralph Raimi further reflected on his own experience in the war,

> By 1940 it became something of a public scandal that Army draftees knew so little of mathematics that the Army itself had to undertake their training in the arithmetic necessary for even the most mundane bookkeeping and gunnery; and by 1945 the deficiency became even more evident when the wartime developments in radar, navigation, operations analysis, cryptography, rockets and atomic weapons (among others) showed the extent of mathematical accomplishment needed for a modern society, at war or at peace. "Practical" mathematics was not just arithmetic and interest rates any more, and whatever it was, America didn't have it. About 1950 there arose the beginnings of an attempt at reform, generated by some previously indifferent mathematicians among others, an attempt that burgeoned when the Soviet Sputnik of 1957 plunged Congress into shock.

Both courses and their teachers were needed, and local autonomy needed to be modified. Before World War II, most Americans lived in towns, not cities. The existence of small high schools in every state led

James B. Conant in his extensive study of American high schools in the 1950s to call for a high school with a graduating class of at least one hundred students. He asserted that "a small high school cannot by its very nature offer a comprehensive curriculum. . . . Financial considerations restrict the course offerings of the small high schools."[15]

Conant advocated a high school of at least four hundred students (his ideal was about seven hundred fifty) so that it could provide specialized programs to meet the needs and interests of a broad range of students. He was particularly concerned about the absence of advanced coursework in mathematics and science. While a small high school could offer such programs, Conant believed that the extravagant cost would ultimately be prohibitive.

Regional high schools had begun to be built after World War II, and Conant's influential book accelerated the movement. Moreover, high school science and mathematics curricula were strengthened. One of Conant's interests was in increasing the number of public school students at the nation's prestigious colleges and universities. What is ironic is that at the very time that the science and mathematics curriculum in the nation's high schools was being strengthened, to develop more public school students with advanced knowledge and skills in mathematics, the English curriculum was being weakened for almost all public school students — although it has rarely been portrayed that way.[16]

KEY IDEAS TO REMEMBER

1. The earliest colonists in New England (the Puritans) considered the provision of children's education one of the major financial obligations of each incorporated community.
2. The ideal of one high school for all children in a community appealed to most Americans.
3. Most public high schools in the nineteenth century served many students who did not intend to go to college even if they did complete high school.
4. To address non-college-intending students' interests, small public high school in the nineteenth century offered many courses in a variety of subjects to small numbers of students.
5. The passage of compulsor school attendance laws across states beginning in Massachusetts in 1852 caused many students to stay on in school. Attendance was further reinforced by Child Labor Laws at the turn of the the twentieth century.
6. The teaching force and curriculum in urban schools were usually superior to those in non-urban schools.
7. Local taxpayers until well after World War II were financially responsible for their public schools.

8. Consolidation of small high schools after WWII helped to strengthen the mathematics and science curriculum. It did not strengthen the English curriculum.

NOTES

1. "The Landscape of Public Education: A Statistical Portrait through the Years," *Epicenter*, April 2011, 5 and figure 10, Number of Male and Female Public High School Graduates, 1940–2008, http://educationalpolicy.org/publications/EPI%20Center/EPICenter_K-12.pdf.
2. https://eh.net/encyclopedia/child-labor-during-the-british-industrial-revolution/
3. https://eh.net/encyclopedia/child-labor-during-the-british-industrial-revolution/
4. Isaac Kandel, *The Dilemma of Democracy* (Cambridge, MA: Harvard University Press, 1934), 26.
5. See the first two chapters in Sandra Stotsky, *Losing Our Language*, original edition published by Free Press, 1999 (New York: Encounter Books, 2002 [reprint]).
6. Jeff Lingwall, *Compulsory Schooling, the Family, and the Foreign Element in the United States, 1880–1900*, 2010. http://www.heinz.cmu.edu/faculty-and-research/research/research-details/index.aspx?rid=372.
7. Edward Krug, "Graduates of Secondary Schools in and around 1900: Did Most of Them Go to College?," *The School Review* 70 (1962): 266–72.
8. National Center for Education Statistics, *Digest of Education Statistics*, 2008, Table 32, Historical Summary of Public Elementary and Secondary School Statistics: Selected Years, 1869–70 through 2005–06, https://nces.ed.gov/programs/digest/d08/tables/dt08_032.asp.
9. http://en.wikipedia.org/wiki/History_of_education_in_the_United_States#Compulsory_laws.
10. http://www.econ.ucla.edu/alleras/research/papers/education_paper-revised2.pdf.
11. For example, the Marvell School District in eastern Arkansas enrolled 179 students in grades nine to twelve in 2009–2010. The Arkansas Department of Education lists sixty-nine different courses being taught, a few for individual students. Among Marvell's course offerings are agricultural mechanics, agricultural metals, and agricultural science and technology, as well as AP English language and composition.
12. Claudia Goldin, "America's Graduation from High School: The Evolution and Spread of Secondary Schooling in the Twentieth Century," *Journal of Economic History*, 1998, 58 (2): 345–74.
13. Kandel, *Dilemma*, 52–53.
14. Ralph Raimi, "Judging State Standards for K–12 Mathematics Education," in *What's at Stake in the K–12 Standards Wars*, ed. Sandra Stotsky (New York: Peter Lang, 2000): 35–36.
15. James B. Conant, *The American High School Today* (New York: McGraw Hill, 1959), 77.
16. See one of those rare examples: David G. Savage, "The Long Decline in SAT Scores," *Educational Leadership*, 1978, http://www.ascd.org/ASCD/pdf/journals/ed_lead/el_197801_savage.pdf.

FOUR
Fragmentation of the English Curriculum in the Twentieth Century

Reading skills heavily influence school attendance, secondary course taking, and academic achievement. They further influence the development of writing skills beyond the early years of schooling, when writing is almost a transcription of a child's speech patterns. The development of reading skills, especially a reading vocabulary, and then writing skills depends largely on practice—willing practice in reading. There are no silver bullets for a large reading vocabulary.

The compulsory education laws and prohibitions against factory work compelled most students to stay in high school—instead of leaving school to work on a family farm or in a family business, serve as an apprentice for a trade, or sign up for military service. By looking at major changes to the English curriculum over the twentieth century, it is possible to discern what educators did to keep students with a minimal interest in reading and studying engaged with schooling.

Before looking at the specific changes that took place in what may have been the first major reorganization of the high school curriculum since its development in the 1600s (the first public school—Boston Latin—was founded in 1635), it is useful to recall that most students were expected to read high school–level books and other adult materials by the time they graduated. Whether or not they were college-intending, a high school diploma meant readiness for the civic responsibilities of adult life—informed citizenship, as it was once called—and the ability to read adult materials and to write in ways that could be understood by an intended reader.

STRUCTURAL CHANGES IN K–12 EDUCATION AT THE TURN OF THE TWENTIETH CENTURY

The surge in high school enrollment at the turn of the twentieth century—mainly reflecting the huge wave of immigration to our urban areas—led educators to make many changes to the high school curriculum as high schools were being built or expanded—in large part to accommodate the wide range of reading skills and student interests in grades ten through twelve.[1] Several sinister theories have long been advanced to account for these changes (e.g., to sort out upper-class children from those who would become part of the workforce). It is probably the case that some education policy makers or community leaders were motivated to make drastic structural changes to the high school curriculum by a desire to sort out future workers from students most suited to manage a capitalistic economy or public affairs.

What is more telling is the general failure of education historians to mention the differences in reading skills among secondary school students and the effects of these differences on the school curriculum. The range in reading skill at any one grade typically goes from many grades above a particular grade level to the same number below it—and widens as one moves up the grades. None of the well-known historians of American education (e.g., Lawrence Cremin, Carl Kaestle, Jeffrey Mirel, Larry Cuban, Diane Ravitch, David Tyack, or Maris Vinovskis) has, to my knowledge, tried to explain the structural changes that took place in the high school curriculum around the turn of the twentieth century from the perspective of a high school teacher, especially the high school English teacher.

Most scholars seem to turn correlation into causation when noting the relationship of ability grouping, achievement grouping, or "tracking" to socioeconomic mobility, income, and college attendance, and then decry its negative effects. But the critics of "grouping" or "tracking" generally avoid discussing the basis for students' initial placement in a low-achievement group or track—usually prior achievement and reading skill.[2]

What and how could teachers teach in a high school or any secondary classroom (grades seven to twelve) if large numbers of students in their class couldn't read the science or history textbooks for their grade level (or primary documents in history) or the assigned texts in an English class for a particular grade level? For a variety of reasons, wealthy parents often took their children, whether or not they were motivated students, out of the public schools after grade eight or nine to enroll them in a private school where extremely small classes (e.g., ten students per teacher) were generally available. The students attending newly formed or expanded high schools were not apt to be the children of the wealthy but the children of the broad middle class and immigrants. It is more likely that thoughtful educators of the time were more concerned with how to retain the enrollment of competent students in the public schools, as well as community support for their public schools, without compromising their civic purposes in a civic culture. Most public schools were funded totally by local taxpayers, as were public libraries—an institution like the comprehensive high school that was voluntarily founded and funded by taxpayers in communities across the country in the latter half of the nineteenth century or at the turn of the century. Educators of the time undoubtedly wanted as many students as possible to attend the community's public schools and as much public support for them as possible. A curriculum track within a comprehensive high school seemed to be the best solution local educators could work out—and it lasted for over half a century.

As education historian Jeffrey Mirel noted, by 1920 most urban high schools had four tracks: college-preparatory, general, vocational (industrial arts/home economics), and commercial. The commercial or business track was popular with girls from low-income families who saw a future job waiting for them as a bookkeeper, salesperson, secretary, or accountant. (More girls than boys attended and graduated from high school until well after World War II.) It is not clear to what extent school administrators and teachers placed students in a "track" after grade eight (or counseled them to enroll in a particular track) or if students actively chose a particular track in the context of their academic interests or family income. Anecdotes differ on the extent of student or family "choice" in this matter among the first-generation of the children of immigrant families (at the turn of the twentieth century) who graduated from their local high school, I have discovered.

Junior high schools also began to be established around the beginning of the twentieth century (pulling out grades seven to nine from a secondary school containing grades seven to twelve or taking grades seven and eight from the "grammar" school, and grade nine from the high school). Classes in grades seven, eight, and nine were typically organized homogeneously, enabling teachers to assign students with strong reading skills books written for adolescents or adults, and to assign less demanding readings to those with weaker reading skills—or to teach them less or at a slower pace. Homogeneous classes were at first considered a reform of a seeming straitjacket—a one-size-fits-all curriculum. The internal pedagogical problem all school districts wrestled with was the growing spread in reading and writing skills. In self-contained elementary classrooms, teachers could and did organize three to five different reading groups, tailor reading instruction to a group's skill needs, and handle topics in subject areas taught to the whole class (e.g., geography) at a level the lowest readers could manage. Once the school curriculum was divided into basic subjects taught by teachers of those subjects in timed periods over the course of a day, usually in grade six or seven, the teaching dilemma began and continued until grade twelve. Students' reading skills rarely evened out by the end of the elementary grades, regardless of the method or instructional reader used.[3]

Students in a high school's college preparatory program always read a demanding range of books, speeches, biographies, and essays. Many large cities also had special high schools for high achievers, like Boston Latin School, Central High School in Philadelphia, Lowell High School in San Francisco, or Dunbar High School in Washington, D.C.[4] Their academic level can be judged by what their able students were expected to read in grades nine through twelve after the first College Board examinations were given, in 1901. The teaching dilemma was what to assign other students.

High school English teachers did not want to lower their own standards or downgrade their goal of literary taste. They had to find books that were appealing to students who weren't highly motivated to read George Eliot's *Silas Marner*, Oliver Goldsmith's *Vicar of Wakefield*, or Edmund Burke's "Speech on Conciliation with the American Colonies"—authors whose vocabulary and sentence structures were decidedly above middle/junior high school reading level and whose works were among the top high school titles in the English curriculum at the turn of the century. As observed by George Tanner, author of a well-known survey of sixty-seven high schools in the Midwest in the first decade of the twentieth century, a wide array of titles was assigned in English classes in these high schools "to meet the various conditions in different schools, and the different personalities of the teachers," instead of a narrow list of College Board–required titles—what he expected. [5]

Despite the intentions of the Committee of Ten in 1892 to establish a demanding curriculum for all high school students, other forces—many associated with the development of American education schools in the next two decades—wanted alternatives to a classical, college-oriented curriculum in order to address better, they thought, the interests of non-college-intending students. Separate vocational schools were established in 1917 with help from the federal government, and their numbers were expanded in 1960.[6] In addition to vocational schools, other kinds of high schools were occasionally developed (for the performing arts or for mathematics and science) over the twentieth century, while magnet schools focusing on a particular occupational area became popular after World War II as a possible way to reduce racial isolation across school district boundaries and improve the achievement of urban low-achieving students. But the setting did not change and has not changed for most students. Most students in most school districts in this country still attend a "comprehensive" high school—an institution unique to this country—whether or not they encounter a socioeconomically narrow range of students in their academic classes.

By the late twentieth century, most curriculum tracks in the "comprehensive" high school had been abolished. In other words, a student could not be placed in or could not choose in one stroke a sequence of courses across a range of disciplines all geared to a lower level of reading and writing than what was expected in an honors or advanced course—or to an occupation requiring certain kinds of reading and writing. Sometimes just the bottom track (of four tracks often labeled basic, standard, honors, and advanced) had been eliminated, or students could choose the level of the course they wanted to take in an individual subject. In order to promote "inclusion" and "self-esteem," students who would have been in a basic or remedial class in grade nine could opt for (or be placed in) a standard or honors-level class.

The effects on the classroom curriculum of having students with poor reading skills in English or history classes together with students with higher reading skills (after the elimination of a bottom level) have not been well researched and documented. However, it is unlikely that students with very low reading skills were now assigned the reading material once assigned to classes of more able readers (one of the hopes of those who favored eliminating the bottom track). It is more likely that teachers assigned less demanding reading material to the whole class, including the more able students, in order to accommodate the low reading level of those now in these classes. While some students may have gained in self-esteem, others lost in intellectual challenge.

Books have been written about the structural changes in the American high school over the course of the twentieth century, the establishment of junior high schools, and then their transformation into middle schools, a movement accelerating after World War II. Critiques have usually analyzed these changes in relation to students' socioeconomic status, especially that of African-Americans. After World War II, homogeneous classes were eliminated in junior high or middle schools in the name of reform in order to reduce the isolation of low achievers, especially if most were identifiable by race. For unclear reasons, such classes seem to have been more thoroughly eliminated in urban schools attended chiefly by minority students than in suburban schools.[7] But the elimination of homogeneous classes in the middle grades may have affected the coherence of the reading/literature curriculum less than did the breakup of the year-long high school English course. Both movements were designed with the interests of low achievers in mind, but both failed to contribute to higher achievement for low-achieving students.

Chapter 4

FRAGMENTATION OF A COHERENT SECONDARY LITERATURE CURRICULUM

Fragmentation began with the break-up of the year-long English course after World War II—usually into a variety of electives. Until then, high school English courses, like courses in most other subjects, were year-long courses. Breaking them into two semester-long courses and into electives was justified by many English teachers as a way to honor individual uniqueness and to give students the opportunity to make choices. It also facilitated increased attention to composition. As at Brookline High School in Massachusetts at the time, for example, many schools required students to choose a literature course for one elective each year, and a writing-oriented course for the other elective.

While no one could deny that student writing needed more attention, and that public school students in general were not given as many writing assignments (to be evaluated by the teacher) as were students in small classes in private schools, the attention now given to composition in a semester-long course was problematic in several ways. It reduced the time for whole-class discussions of assigned literary or nonliterary texts and it was *never* the case that intellectual benefits from the increased time allotted to composition were demonstrated on a large scale (e.g., on NAEP tests of writing). Spending a lot of instructional time in class on writing had trade-offs that warranted discussion, but such discussions cannot be located in professional education journals.

The conversion of junior high schools into middle schools—beginning about 1970—delivered a second blow to curriculum coherence and quality. The motivation behind the development of middle schools and yet another reorganization of the secondary curriculum was similar to the basic motivation behind the high school electives movement—the desire to arouse the interest of non-academically oriented young adolescents in reading, especially students who didn't read much. So far as we can tell now—that is, in retrospect—the major result of the structural "reform" known as the middle school movement was the eventual replacement over time of academically qualified teachers in grades seven and eight by academically under-qualified teachers (often an elementary teacher who had "added" whatever the state required for earning a middle school license—sometimes no more than a course in adolescent development).

The conversion of junior high schools (typically for grades seven to nine) to middle schools (many with grades four or five to eight) allowed the curriculum in grades seven and eight to become the culmination of an elementary school curriculum rather than the grounding for secondary subject matter learning as in a school of grades seven to twelve or in a junior high school. This was clearer in mathematics than in English. Algebra I, preceded by a course called pre-Algebra, could be suitable for grades seven and eight or grades eight and nine in a junior high school, but less so for grades seven and eight in a middle school. (Algebra I was the gateway for advanced math courses in high school, not the culmination of a math curriculum for a grade eight graduation from a grammar school.) Moreover, a teacher capable of teaching algebra was more likely to be in a junior high school than in a middle school.

We have not yet, in this country, worked out better academic solutions to the increasing range of interests and reading skills in young adolescents than either the junior high school or the middle school seems to have provided as educational institutions. However, the splitting of the year-long high school English class into two semester-long electives, and the conversion of the junior high school to a middle school did reduce, in at least two different ways, the instructional time English teachers once spent developing thinking skills by means of whole-class discussion of challenging reading assignments given to the whole class.

Turning the year-long English class into two semester-long electives enabled teachers so inclined to ignore the spread in students' reading levels for a semester-long course oriented to composition and to assign a sequence of writing assignments, many of which were autobiographical in content, unrelated to any reading assignment for the whole class (if there were any). A tinge of ideology crept in as defense for speech-based or experience-based composition courses. On theoretical grounds it was more egalitarian to posit relationships between writing and speaking than between writing and reading because all children grew up to speak the language of their community without formal lessons. On disciplinary grounds, it also seemed to make sense. As a faculty member at SUNY-Albany commented, "Until the 1970s, writing and reading were not conceptualized as being integrated. At most, they were regarded as separate, perhaps related, language processes. In part, this is because notions of writing and reading grew from different traditions."[8]

Moreover, achievement grouping came to be seen as a moral evil. Grouping students without regard to reading level was seen as more "democratic" and justified as promoting more learning than achievement grouping did, even though research evidence is actually quite mixed on this issue. See the studies mentioned in a 2011 article, for example.[9]

The work of James Moffett (from the 1960s on) was significant in this respect. It is hard to overestimate Moffett's influence on English education in the middle to latter half of the twentieth century, especially on individual English teachers.[10] His focus was on reform of the English curriculum in order to stress the development of thought (thinking skills) and understanding (comprehension) through language. He sought to develop a sequence of writing activities over the years originating in oral language activities. As James Squire, at one time director of the National Council of Teachers of English and later editor in chief of a major publishing company, commented in a foreword to Moffett's 1968 handbook for teachers, "For many pupils power in reading is closely associated with power in writing and speech."[11]

Moffett's ideas on how to sequence writing assignments were theoretically elegant. His organizing principles substituted the changing psychological distance of a speaker/writer from the subject and audience of his/her composition for the four long-used "modes" of discourse in teaching secondary writing: description, narration, exposition, and persuasion. Moffett's views on language and learning captured the attention of many curriculum developers. Moffett had worked out his ideas when teaching very able students at a demanding private school in New Hampshire, and his ideas seemed to assume, at the least, willing readers in secondary schools. How his ideas could be adapted (and why they needed to be adapted) for students in a range of public high schools should have been discussed cogently at conferences for English teachers, but they were not. Growing numbers of elementary and secondary teachers from the 1980s on, as the writing process movement swept the country, seem to have been more interested in an acceptable or prestigious rationale for student-centered writing and students' choice of what they read grounded in student motivation rather than in language learning and the development of thinking.

Perhaps more damaging to the coherence of a reading/literature curriculum through the grades than allying reading to speaking activities was an insistence by those educators interested in student growth (e.g., James Britton in England) on student choice of what they read. No planned curriculum is possible if students choose what they want to study in the English class. Most English teachers still wanted some useful principles for organizing their school or classroom reading/literature curriculum. Moffett didn't offer anything as specific as what he had laid out for developing writing and for moving students from narrative writing (organized in large part by chronology) to essay writing (organized rationally by a thesis or controlling idea—always an intellectual hurdle for the students of a grade nine English teacher) primarily because he was against "curriculum-driven" teaching.[12] His *Teaching the Universe of Discourse*, first published in 1968, suggested that "student-centered" teaching was to draw on a set of individualized activities promoting a student's intellectual and emotional growth.

But because this kind of individualized teaching was not possible in schools where English teachers saw over one hundred students every week, maybe twenty-five or more per class, five different classes every day, sometimes one hundred fifty students per week, the reading and literature curriculum in many school districts of necessity came to be organized in the secondary grades mainly by the range of genres that students were to be exposed to (and sometimes by popular political themes), not by the cultural, historical, or aesthetic connections that specific works had to each other, by literary periods or movements, or by their increasing difficulty and complexity as individual texts. It is almost impossible to find a set of reading/literature standards for our public schools (or for the college-preparatory "track") that are as specific or as demanding as the specifications for secondary English in academically oriented private schools to this day (see, for example, the required titles in the English curriculum for the Brearley School in Manhattan or for the Sidwell School in Washington, D.C.[13]).

Exposure to a differing range of genres for speech and writing through the grades (not specific titles, authors, movements, or periods) became a popular way to organize the secondary reading/literature curriculum, and it is still in vogue. The textbook/handbook that James Moffett and Betty Jane Wagner coauthored for classroom teachers and English education courses in education schools went through four editions. Originally authored by Moffett in 1968 and titled *A Student-Centered Language Arts Curriculum, Grades K–13: A Handbook for Teachers*, the fourth edition of the coauthored textbook (published in 1992) is described online in the following way: "The essentials of the approach they advocate no longer need justification—having been adopted in the last decade under such rubrics as whole language, reading in the content areas, writing across the curriculum, using language to learn, integrating the language arts, replacing basal readers with children's literature, cooperative learning and collaborative learning, process writing and process reading, writing response groups, peer editing, portfolio assessment, teacher-student conferencing, student empowerment, active learning, and critical thinking. Increasingly, verbal learning is allied to nonverbal media and arts that compete with and complement language, and all learning is placed in a social context."[14]

Probably the best account of Moffett's contribution to English education is by Sheridan Blau, a professor of literature and teaching methods in English education, in a commemorative essay written in 2010.[15] His essay provides a "history and evaluation of James Moffett's shaping influence on the way composition and its teaching are understood theoretically and how teachers learn to teach writing through the National Writing Project."

In light of the academic acclaim and pedagogical acceptance of the teaching practices that Moffett and Wagner recommended for the English language arts, one must wonder why most governors and state boards and departments of education adopted almost sight unseen in 2010 the English language arts standards known as Common Core. These standards were developed chiefly by two people (David Coleman and Sue Pimentel) who had never taught literary study or composition or other language arts at any educational level (i.e., they had no work-related credentials). Nor did state decision makers typically consult with English teachers on the adoption of these standards. Unsurprisingly, Congress, parents, and the public at large have no idea why all the practices now apparently "justified" by the National Council of Teachers of English (NCTE) and English educators have resulted in average student achievement levels in 2015 that are not very different from those in the 1970s on the "Nation's Report Cards." Practices designed to strengthen the education of low achievers by motivating them, as described in Moffett's writings and NCTE's professional literature, seem to have failed all children, including low achievers.

It is possible that the virtual disappearance of Moffett's ideas from the arsenal of influential ideas in English education departments in education schools and from the thinking of curriculum developers in district school offices for K–12 may be accounted for by the dominance of "the writing process" as advocated from the 1970s on by Donald Graves and his best-known acolyte Lucy Calkins.[16] Moffett's focus on writing may, in retrospect, be seen as the harbinger of a change in the school curriculum that altered the amount of attention paid to all the other language arts and maybe other subjects as well.

Education researchers wouldn't be able to pick up what was changing in the instructional day without systematic observations to find out if and how elementary or middle school teachers had altered the use of their instructional time to include the "writing process." Writing as composing was as much a part of the package of the language arts to be taught as were reading, speaking, spelling, handwriting, writing conventions, vocabulary development, and listening (and more).

By the mid-1970s, the emphasis on teaching writing had captured many teachers' imagination and instructional time. We cannot know how much instructional time on average was used by elementary teachers for setting up "the author's chair," encouraging revisions and multiple drafts based on peer comments, and giving "mini-lessons" on writing skills without extensive observational research, of which there seems to have been little. To expand the amount of class time normally spent on composing, teachers had to take time from something already being taught because the school day was never lengthened anywhere for teachers to teach writing through an elaborate writing process and—since the 1990s and 2000s—to prepare students for annual state tests as well.

The problem in trying to find out if and how large-scale instructional shifts within the language arts took place was compounded by the claim of many teachers and publishers that the other language arts, including reading, were being taught through writing as part of an "integrated" process set forth in their instructional materials and in professional development. But how much instructional time teachers actually used for the other language arts or how it was "integrated" has rarely been recorded by education researchers.[17]

In a 1979 study that documented what teachers in six elementary classrooms did in teaching what they were expected to teach, and the language arts in particular, over a twelve-week period, the researchers found that the time spent in language arts instruction, especially writing instruction, varied considerably from day to day and from teacher to teacher. Yet, in a 1997 report on time spent on core subjects, researchers did not find teachers reporting major differences across schools in the amount of time spent on core subjects.[18] Not surprising. Since writing was part of a core subject, a shift in emphasis on a particular language art would not have shown up.

Time to generate ideas, draft, revise, redraft, revise, edit, and publish became a sacrosanct part of the language arts period after the 1980s. It could always be argued (and was) that students did need to learn how to write better and that teachers themselves needed to learn how to write better (hence, the development of the National Writing Project). But researchers trying to determine how teachers use instructional time would not find out how much time had been spent on any of the language arts, including writing, if their classification system didn't allow for a shift in time spent on components within a core subject as multifaceted as the language arts.

This is similar to the problem we face in knowing how much time teachers spend on "teaching to the test." Mostly we have self-report surveys. While some researchers have found many teachers reporting that they spend a lot of instructional time (or too much) on test preparation,[19] others have found large numbers of teachers reporting that they can justify what they do, as in this 2016 report.[20]

FURTHER WEAKENING OF A COHERENT ENGLISH CURRICULUM

An insistence on student-centered writing and student choice of reading might have been accommodated in ways that didn't weaken what all students read in secondary school English classes—and consequently everything students read in other classes as well. Broad groups of choices could have been worked out if educators and public policy spokespersons had thought it was important for most high school students to be challenged to read high school–level literary or nonliterary texts before they graduated from high school.

Possessed by the notion that low achievers in certain ethnic groups would be more motivated to read texts about and by people who looked or talked like them, but at the same time believing that poor readers couldn't read the difficult titles required by College Board exams, educators gradually replaced more difficult works in the secondary English curriculum with easier books with respect to vocabulary, syntactic challenge, and ideational complexity on the grounds that existing works were by dead white males, Eurocentric, or reflective of an oppressive culture (British, American, or European). Older, or "canonical," works (almost anything written before 1970) were regularly discredited and replaced by more contemporary works, usually by an ethnically identifiable author. The result: it is difficult to find a currently popular contemporary work assigned in high school that is as difficult to read with respect to its vocabulary and syntax as the "canonical" work it may have displaced.

For example, most students today read *The Watsons Go to Birmingham*, a middle-grade novel with a grade-five reading level, and *To Kill a Mockingbird*, but most students no longer read *The Adventures of Tom Sawyer* and *The Scarlet Letter*. The *Watsons* is about a black family that travels from Flint to Birmingham in 1963, while the original version of *Tom Sawyer* (with a grade-eight reading level) was once a staple in a middle-grade English class. *To Kill a Mockingbird* is a gripping tale narrated by a child about bigotry in a small Southern town in the 1920s and is often taught (for the first time) in grade eight or nine (its reading level is estimated to be at a grade-six level.) On the other hand, *The Scarlet Letter*, about adultery in an early New England Puritan community, was once a staple in a grade-eleven course in American literature but is rarely taught in high school today (its reading level is estimated to be at a grade-eleven level).

It's unlikely that educators promoting what they called "multicultural" literature sought to weaken the literature curriculum for black students. They wanted to motivate them, elevate their status, and promote their self-esteem. But no researcher has found a positive effect on student reading interest from eliminating what was denigrated as "canonical" works. (Other cultural forces, including watching TV and playing video games, may have negatively affected the time students spent in leisure reading, but no research has uncovered a positive effect from the introduction of whatever was designated as "multicultural" literature.)

According to Renaissance Learning, a company that produces a program called Accelerated Reader, now in thousands of low-income schools or their curriculum libraries across the country, the average reading level of the top twenty-five titles assigned to or read by grade-eleven students is at about the grade-six level.[21] Students in an Advanced Placement English course may still read high school–level or adult texts, but the College Board does not require specific titles for this course. As a result, the variation across approved syllabi precludes generalizations about reading levels for even the most advanced readers in high school.

Research is now being done on a recent strategy called "personalized learning." So far, there is not much to be excited about, according to a 2016 overview of the research.[22] "Personalized learning" seems to a warmed-over version of decades-old "individualized instruction," but with technology use added. No information is yet available on what high school students actually read before they graduate.[23]

KEY IDEAS TO REMEMBER

1. Development of a large reading vocabulary is the key to reading skills. College-level reading material (written by academic experts) has traditionally assumed high school-level reading and vocabulary skills.
2. High school graduates have traditionally been expected to read high school-level or adult reading material for informed citizenship whether or not college-intending.
3. A huge high school expansion at the turn of the twentieth century reflected large waves of immigration to this country, especially its cities. The need to retain many students without strong interests/skills in reading but compelled by child labor laws and compulsory schooling laws to stay in school was a major reason for the reorganization of the high school curriculum.
4. The reading curriculum for non-college-intending students was altered by "curriculum tracks" and by the establishment of junior high schools for grades 7, 8, and 9 in place of a traditional 8–4 system.
5. After WWII, curriculum tracks were abolished in many high schools, junior high schools were converted to middle schools, and the reading level of high school textbooks was reduced.
6. From the 1970s on, the writing process movement and the integration of language arts spread through elementary schools. No evidence has ever been presented that most students learned to read and write better.
7. The K–8 curriculum in the last half of the twentieth century promoted student choice of reading texts and student-centered writing. The reading level of all students gradually declined.
8. Multiculturalism (the belief that the history and literature of all cultures or groups of people were of equal worth in the curriculum) also led to easier reading material—and further decline in the reading level of average high school graduates.

NOTES

1. Jeffrey Mirel, "The Traditional High School: Historical Debates over its Nature and Function," *Education Next*, 2006, 6 (1), http://educationnext.org/the-traditional-high-school/. See Figure 1 on enrollment changes from 1900–2000.

2. William Morrison, "High School Curriculum Tracks as Determinants of Post-Secondary Outcomes: A Study of Track Mobility and Its Effects," 2013, Dissertations, Paper 728, http://ecommons.luc.edu/cgi/viewcontent.cgi?article=1727&context=luc_diss.

3. Lisa Stein, "Tracking Texts: Designing Innovations to Enhance Reading Comprehension," 2007, http://www.sesp.northwestern.edu/news-center/inquiry/2007-spring/tracking-texts.html.

4. For a history of Dunbar High School, see http://www.blackpast.org/aah/paul-laurence-dunbar-high-school-1870.

5. George Tanner, "Report of the Committee Appointed by the English Conference to Inquire into the Teaching of English in the High Schools of the Middle West," *School Review*, 1907, 15: 37–45.

6. See "Smith Hughes Act," https://www.britannica.com/topic/Smith-Hughes-Act, for a brief history of the movement to establish vocational schools in 1917 and the wide array of social, business, and other groups supporting these schools.

7. See Tom Loveless, "Ability Grouping, Tracking, and How Schools Work," April 3, 2013, https://www.brookings.edu/research/ability-grouping-tracking-and-how-schools-work/. For a research-based discussion, see Tom Loveless, *Tracking and Detracking: High Achievers in Massachusetts Middle Schools*, Thomas B. Fordham Institute, December 2009, http://www.schoolinfosystem.org/pdf/2009/12/200912_Detracking.pdf.

8. Judith A. Langer and Sheila Flihan, "Writing and Reading Relationships: Constructive Tasks," in *Writing: Research/Theory/Practice*, ed. Roselmina Indrisano and James R. Squire (Newark, DE: International Reading Association, 2000),http://www.albany.edu/cela/publication/article/writeread.htm.

9. Michael J. Petrilli, "All Together Now? Educating High and Low Achievers in the Same Classroom," *Education Next*, 2011, 11 (1), http://educationnext.org/all-together-now/.

10. Michael Michaud, "Democratizing Writing: Reflections on the Great Revolution: A Conversation with Thomas Newkirk," *Composition Forum 32*, 2015, http://compositionforum.com/issue/32/thomas-newkirk-interview.php. For brief reviews of James Moffett's major writings, see https://www.nwp.org/cs/public/print/resource/102.

11. James Squire, Foreword in James Moffett *A Language-Centered Language Arts Curriculum, Grades K–12: A Handbook for Teachers* (Boston: Houghton Mifflin, 1968): vii.

12. http://www.csun.edu/~krowlands/Content/Academic_Resources/Reading/Useful%20Articles/moffett%20and%20wagner-reading.pdf.

13. James Moffett and Betty Jane Wagner, "Student-Centered Activities," *The English Journal* 80 (6) 70–73, http://www.csun.edu/~krowlands/Content/Academic_Resources/Reading/Useful%20Articles/moffett%20and%20wagner-reading.pdf.

14. https://www.amazon.com/Student-Centered-Language-Arts-James-Moffett/dp/0867092920.

15. https://www.researchgate.net/publication/282826405_Theory_for_PracticeJames_Moffett%27s_Seminal_Contributionn_to_Composition.

16. Sheridan Blau, "Theory for Practice: James Moffett's Seminal Contribution to Composition," https://www.researchgate.net/publication/282826405_Theory_for_PracticeJames_Moffett%27s_Seminal_Contributionn_to_Composition, in *Composition's Roots in English Education*, ed. Patricia Lambert Stock (Portsmouth, NH: Boynton Cook, 2010).

17. Tribute to Donald H. Graves, https://www.heineman.com/authors/998.aspx, and Lucy McCormick Calkins, *The Art of Teaching Writing* (flyer), https://www.amazon.com/Teaching-Writing-Lucy-McCormick-Calkins/dp/0435088092.

18. Laura Roehler, William Schmidt, and Margaret Buchmann, *How Do Teachers Spend Their Language Arts Time?*, Institute for Research on Teaching, Research Series NO. 66, Michigan State University, December 1979, https://education.msu.edu/irt/PDFs/ResearchSeries/rs066.pdf.

19. Marianne Perie, David P. Baker, and Sharon Bobbitt, *Time Spent Teaching Core Academic Subjects in Elementary Schools: Comparisons across Community, School, Teacher, and Student Characteristics*, National Center for Education Statistics: A Statistical Analysis Report, February 1997, https://nces.ed.gov/pubs/97293.pdf.

20. Eric Robelen, "Testing and Test Prep: How Much Is Too Much?" EWA, June 3, 2016, http://www.ewa.org/blog-educated-reporter/testing-and-test-prep-how-much-too-much.

21. Mark Teoh, et al., *The Best of Time or the Worst of Time: What Teachers Think about Test Preparation*, Teach Plus, Spring 2016, http://www.teachplus.org/sites/default/files/publication/pdf/test_prep_report.pdf.

22. Benjamin Herold, "Personalized Learning: What Does the Research Say?," *Education Week*, October 18, 2016, http://www.edweek.org/ew/articles/2016/10/19/personalized-learning-what-does-the-research-say.html/.

23. http://k12education.gatesfoundation.org/resource/personalized-learning-helping-teachers-spark-a-love-of-learning-in-every-student/; http://k12education.gatesfoundation.org/resource/investing-in-the-promise-of-quality-personalized-learning/.

FIVE

Evolving Explanations of Low Achievement

How Well Education Programs and Strategies Have Addressed It

It is startling to review the evolution of explanations for low achievement and to understand current explanations. Rarely do education policy makers or researchers point a finger at a lack of interest in reading—or a limited reading vocabulary—as a characteristic of low achievers even though many teachers see limited vocabulary knowledge as the foremost reason for a student's low academic achievement.

A wide range of interventions (education programs and strategies) have been developed to address low achievement as it is now conceptualized, with little or no success. Massive low achievement has not yet been susceptible to education solutions. This chapter examines one probably influential description of "factors that contribute to achievement gaps," and reviews the range of education interventions that have tried to address these "gaps" in some way whether or not they were developed expressly for that purpose.

"FACTORS CONTRIBUTING TO ACHIEVEMENT GAPS" ACCORDING TO THE NEA

The National Education Association (NEA) has prepared a chart in a pamphlet dated 2017 of what it sees as "factors that contribute to achievement gaps" "within" and "outside schools' control."[1] It lists the following factors as within school influence in the chart (copied as they appear):

Schoolwide Factors

> low expectations for student achievement;
> lack of rigor in the curriculum;
> large class size;
> tracking groups of students into a less demanding curriculum;
> unsafe schools;
> culturally unfriendly environments; and
> poor, or no, instructional leadership.

Teacher and Teaching-Related Factors

> uncertified and inexperienced teachers;
> insensitivity to different cultures;
> poor teacher preparation;
> low expectations of students; and
> inadequate materials, equipment, and resources, including technology-based resources.

Student-Related Factors

> students' interest in school;
> students' level of effort; and
> students' feeling that they are, in part, responsible for their learning

Families' Support of Student Learning

> families' participation in school activities;
> families' skills to support and reinforce learning; and
> students' TV watching and at-home reading.

School and teacher-related traits are first and second, suggesting that they carry more weight than student willingness to study or do homework. Families seem to be responsible for students' "at-home reading," the only instance in which reading is mentioned. Factors outside school control for the family include: "Time family members are able to devote to support and reinforce learning. Other Factors Societal bias (racial, ethnic, poverty and class)."

The NEA goes so far as to imply that if students feel in any way they are responsible for their learning (something they were regularly told in the 1960s that they were responsible for), they are contributing to their own low achievement. Today's low achievers have chiefly their schools, teachers, and society at large to blame for the gaps, this NEA pamphlet implies, and should see others responsible for their low achievement.

A host of questions bubble up. Does cultivating such an attitude towards their teachers, schools, and family help low achievers to improve in school? Should teachers try to imply to students that their families or teachers are in large part responsible for their low achievement? Improvement seems unlikely to be the goal of this blame-game; more money for the schools does.

It is common sense that most of the factors mentioned could, individually or together, contribute to low achievement. But it is also the case that, singly or together, they don't prevent students from reading.

It is also the case that it is difficult to find as a cause of low achievement in the NEA document either precise definitions or examples of most of the concepts listed as causative factors. No references point to research on any one of these factors. The list was made up. For example, what is an example of "cultural insensitivity" or "poor leadership" or "poor teacher preparation"? Where is the research or the anecdote showing the broad effects of any of these concepts on achievement? Or are these concepts there to galvanize requests for more funds for (e.g., "retraining") teachers or administrators?

The NEA list reflects a remarkable evolution in half a century in how a society is to understand and address low achievement—beyond simply claiming that "poverty" or a student's language is a factor. Low achievement seems to have become a condition caused by others. High achievement, on the other hand, may apparently be bought by students' parents—by their socio-economic status. It is not earned by students' own efforts. Low achievement in middle-income families or high achievement in low-income families becomes inexplicable.

Student effort as a cause of low achievement seems to be a leftover from the nineteenth century. It's on the list most likely because the NEA didn't know how else to indicate the student's willingness to read. It can't be done by someone else.

NEA's list does imply that a different home language (which is outside of school control) could contribute to "gaps." Asian Americans have known for years that isn't so. But NEA thinks it contributes to low achievement. Fortunately, NEA does not link it to "class."

After World War II (WWII), low achievement was often seen as a reflection of language differences resulting from class differences, and American society was viewed as static, with little or no change in an individual's socio-economic status from one generation to another. Sociologist Basil Bernstein in England famously suggested that differences in child-rearing language patterns between middle and working class parents could be characterized as differences between restricted codes and elaborated codes.[2]

This distinction was soon seen as explanatory and shaded into a language deficit model; low achievement was a reflection of a child's language and an outcome of sluggish language growth. This explanation soon disappeared from educators' vocabulary, perhaps because it seemed to be "blaming the victim," the child's family.

Chapter 5

STRATEGIES OR PROGRAMS TO ADDRESS LOW ACHIEVEMENT

Has low achievement been remedied by any of the strategies or programs educators or policy makers have promoted and tried out since 1965? Changes in the content of the reading/literature curriculum haven't enhanced student achievement, so far as we know.

1. Changes in the Reading Curriculum Haven't Made a Difference

There are no known research studies with generalizable results based on an examination of changes in literary or non-literary content for low achievers at any grade level. One can find "case" studies or anecdotes but no findings in the form of titles that student groups have read over time, with progress in reading difficulty levels.

Since the adoption of Common Core's English language arts standards by most states in 2010, most schools have tried to provide at least a 50/50 balance between literary and "informational" texts in the language arts curriculum from K-12. (There is no evidence that such a balance in the language arts curriculum improves the academic achievement of any group of students.) There is no authoritative research on how successfully English teachers have achieved this balance at any grade level, although they have reported on NAEP surveys a change in the focus of their reading/literature curriculum. [3]

Researchers have used different ways to judge the extent of implementation. After presenting his own method for determining implementation of this change in the reading curriculum in recent years and an analysis of the NAEP results in 2015 for reading and mathematics, Tom Loveless at the Brookings Institution asserted:

> The 2015 NAEP scores were a political disaster for Common Core. Eighth grade math scores, for example, fell for the first time in NAEP'S twenty-five year history (down three points) . . . yes, nonadopters performed better than CCSS states, but only by declining less, not through improved performance. None of the states are setting the world on fire. Whatever is depressing NAEP scores appears to be more general than the impact of one set of standards or another.

2. Pre-School Programs Haven't Made Significant Long-Term Differences

How about all the pre-school programs that have been federally funded for decades? For pre-school programs, we find a few vague hints of effectiveness in a 2017 report titled "The Current State of Scientific Knowledge on Pre-Kindergarten Effects" by an interdisciplinary group of scientists who reviewed the evidence on the impact of state-funded pre-kindergarten programs.[4] The reviewers summarized their work as follows:

Convincing evidence shows that children attending a diverse array of state and school district pre-k programs are more ready for school at the end of their pre-k year than children who do not attend pre-k. Improvements in academic areas such as literacy and numeracy are most common; the smaller number of studies of social-emotional and self-regulatory development generally show more modest improvements in those areas.

Convincing evidence on the longer-term impacts of scaled-up pre-k programs on academic outcomes and school progress is sparse, precluding broad conclusions. The evidence that does exist often shows that pre-k-induced improvements in learning are detectable during elementary school, but studies also reveal null or negative longer-term impacts for some programs.

The reviewers apparently couldn't tease out factors that can be generalized as contributing to effectiveness. But they do imply that there may be some (unnamed) problems lurking in these pre-school programs. After reading this study, a pediatrician concluded: "Our current knowledge is insufficient to justify a large expansion of pre-K as the best path forward." And " . . . despite decades of study, there still really is no or very little evidence of effectiveness beyond the actual preschool year."[5]

Despite outcries about budgetary attempts to curtail pre-school programs, the call seems to be not a halt to funding pre-school programs, just a halt to a "large expansion." It is not clear why an outside evaluation cannot be built into the funds of every large-scale federally funded preschool effort, especially if "longer-term negative impacts" have been detected in some programs and might be addressable in short-term programs.

For example, only with an outside, independent evaluation *might* it be possible to begin to understand the current charge that Boston Latin School (for grades 7-12) lacks diversity in student enrollment[6] in the context of the glowing 2017 evaluation of Boston's pre-school programs.[7] (Admission to Boston Latin School is based chiefly on external, independent exams given in grades 6 and 8.) It is not clear from media accounts of the claim of lack of diversity at Boston Latin why so few black or Hispanic students pass the exam, given the presence of strong pre-school and "Advanced Grade 5" programs in Boston's elementary schools.[8]

The word "might" is used because it is not clear that Congress has even a mild interest in whether or not the funds it appropriates for low-achieving students in any education program today are effective. Some members of Congress seem to be incapable of accepting negative evaluations of the programs Congress supports and of asking for fresh or new ideas. Others may feel that just appropriating the money is enough to show good will towards low-achieving students even if the program damages them or their teachers on a long-term basis.

3. Teacher Professional Development Hasn't Made a Significant Difference

The lack of a relationship between teacher professional development and student achievement is particularly acute in the argument about continued funding of Title II in ESSA in the forthcoming federal budget.[9] Most of Title II funds are for the professional development of teachers of low-achieving students, but credible reviews of professional development have found it almost uniformly ineffective for all teachers with respect to gains in student achievement. Dated 2014, a short report by the Instructional Research Group at the Southeast Regional Educational Laboratory had the following to say about the few studies of mathematics professional development that could be examined, of all those identified in the search:

> Of the 910 studies identified in the search for "effectiveness studies" of math professional development approaches, 643 examined interventions related to math in grades K–12 and were conducted in the United States. Of the 643 studies, the 32 studies listed in this appendix focused primarily on math professional development provided to teachers and used a research design for examining effectiveness. Five of those were determined to have met What Works Clearinghouse evidence standards (version 2.1). . . . And of those five, only two found positive effects on students' math proficiency.

> Thus, there is very limited causal evidence to guide districts and schools in selecting a math professional development approach or to support developers' claims about their approaches. The limited research on effectiveness means that schools and districts cannot use evidence of effectiveness alone to narrow their choice. Instead, they must use their best judgment until more causal evidence becomes available.[10]

An earlier review of the research on professional development in mathematics education reached a similar conclusion. The National Mathematics Advisory Panel (about twenty nationally recognized scholars, educators, researchers, and mathematicians) was charged with, among other things, making recommendations based on the best available scientific evidence on "the training, selection, placement, and professional development of teachers of mathematics in order to enhance students' learning of mathematics."[11] A subcommittee developed criteria for "high quality research" on education.[12]

A Task Group on Teachers and Teacher Education examined all the relevant research brought to its attention by Abt Associates, a consulting agency for research and program implementation hired to locate this research using these criteria.[13] Here is what the Task Group concluded:

> Overall, the Task Group was not able to draw conclusions about the features of professional development that have an impact on students' achievement because of the paucity of studies that investigated this

link. For the studies the Task Group did identify that probed this connection, specificity is lacking regarding the features of the professional development programs where effects were found.

The Task Group uncovered no studies . . . of sufficient quality where the designs and measures permitted them to ask and answer questions about teachers' learning. Most studies used a simple pre- and posttest design with no comparison group or used self-report data on teachers' learning. To ascertain the impact of professional development on students' achievement, the Task Group did identify a small number of studies, but overall, these did not support any specific claims about the nature of professional development that affects teachers' effectiveness.

Occasionally, a review appears and claims professional development is effective in raising student achievement.[14] But the reviewers do not explain why the studies used in their reviews for the meta-analysis of their findings have been deemed unusable according to the professional criteria used by other reviewers (in one case, criteria developed by the staff at What Works Clearinghouse; in the other, criteria developed by the twenty or so scholars and researchers on the National Mathematics Advisory Panel and used by Abt Associates—a highly regarded consultant organization).

Reporters rarely if ever ask teachers whether they wanted the professional development they have been given because they know the answer is apt to be negative, so it is not surprising that studies find it is as disliked as it is ineffective.[15] But if a budget office, federal, state, or local, proposes eliminating programs that are ineffective, Congressional howls are heard. Apparently, some members of Congress prefer to appropriate money for ineffective and possibly damaging education programs for low-achieving students rather than seek out the reasons for the damage.[16]

4. Home Visits Haven't Made a Significant Difference

How about programs for home visits by teachers or other school personnel? Again, we are fortunate to have a 2017 study funded by the federal government titled "Home Visiting Evidence of Effectiveness Review" As the researchers carefully state in their Executive Summary: "First, research evidence of program model effectiveness is limited. As noted earlier, many models do not have high- or moderate-quality studies of their effectiveness; thus, policymakers and program administrators cannot determine whether those models are effective . . . " "Second, more evidence is needed about the effectiveness of home visiting models for different types of families with a range of characteristics . . . " [17]

Dr. Karen Effrem commented on this 2017 study, too: "Data from HomVEE—a federally conducted review of home visiting programs which studies their effects in a number of realms, including child development (related to school readiness and discussion of pre-school strategies), child abuse prevention, and health outcomes—show that these programs are just not very effective." [18] One can imagine the Congressional howls if these programs were on the federal budget maker's chopping block, too.

5. Smaller Classes or Longer School Days/Years Overall Haven't Made a Significant Difference

What about the benefits of smaller classes or longer school days or years for low achievers? Looking specifically at the benefits of smaller classes for low achievers, nationally known researchers have found less benefit for them in smaller classes than in larger classes (in both cases, classes not targeted to low achievers).[19] But that finding hasn't dampened the enthusiasm of those who argue for smaller classes for low achievers.

On the other hand, skeptics of a longer school day (often described as Extended Learning Time or ELT) can find evidence for and against ELT in reviews of longer or more school days—both extensions amounting to more instructional time.[20] Much depends on what is in a longer school day or year but in itself a longer school day (or year) is not a panacea for improving low achievement. Most reviews conclude that the findings are mixed.[21] Moreover, according to a general 2004 review (not focused on low achievement), "research does not show a strong relationship at the cross-national level between achievement test scores and amount of instructional time."[22]

Perhaps more time on homework matters? A 2017 article by researchers at the Brookings Institution didn't find evidence in what they did look at to account for the racial gap "in time spent on homework." So, without evidence they chose to believe that "viewing homework as an outcome of the culture of the school and the expectations of teachers, rather than an outcome of a student's effort" may account for the gap. Aside from implying that most school administrators and teachers are bigots, the researchers assumed that massive low achievement as a result of doing less homework could be explained by low expectations.[23]

So far there has been little research on whether a longer school day or year (one of many ways to make more instructional time available to low achievers) helps low achievers to close the achievement gap and studies of ELT often include a longer school day or year with studies of longer school days. Is it more instructional time that low achievers need (assuming that many of them are simply slower learners) or do they need something different or something different along with more instructional time?

6. Test-Based Retention in Grade 3 May Be Useful

So far, it seems that holding students back in grade 3 may be helpful. Although a Florida-based study of "The Effects of Test-Based Retention on Student Outcomes over Time," published in 2013, found that "the achievement gains from test-based retention fade out over time ... and are statistically insignificant after six years,"[24] it is not yet clear if the students retained in Florida will also experience long-run benefits (compared to former peers now one year/grade ahead of them). While, according to the researchers, "early grade retention could generate benefits that outweigh the opportunity costs," to what extent retained students will still be low achievers in relation to their new peers is unknown.

7. Community Schools May Not Be a Panacea — But Too Soon To Tell

If longer school days or years, smaller classes, and test-based retention in grade 3 don't necessarily make low achievers higher achievers, are full-service or community schools a possible answer? While it is too soon for long-term results from a large number of full-service schools, one can find case studies of such schools with positive findings for "well-implemented" schools.[25] However, parents and researchers may reasonably worry that only when a community school shows higher achievement for its low achievers will its programs be judged "well-implemented."

One well-known study suggests that full-service schools may not necessarily be the answer.[26] The two authors suggest that a better community as measured by poverty rate does not significantly raise test scores if school quality remains basically unchanged. They conclude the Abstract of their study titled "Are High-Quality Schools Enough to Increase Achievement among the Poor? Evidence from the Harlem Children's Zone" as follows:

> We conclude with evidence that suggests high-quality schools are enough to significantly increase academic achievement among the poor. Community programs appear neither necessary nor sufficient . . .

8. Increases in School Personnel Since the 1950s Haven't Made a Significant Difference

What about the increase in personnel in our public schools, a phenomenon that has been called a "staffing surge"? Can that increase be correlated in any way with increased achievement for low achievers? Since the 1950s, schools have added teaching aides as well as reading and mathematics coaches or "lead" teachers to their personnel roster, in addition to a wide range of administrators and other personnel like data managers. Results? As a 2017 study[27] indicates,

From fiscal year (FY) 1950 to FY 2015, the earliest and most recent years with available data, American public schools added full-time equivalent (FTE) personnel at a rate almost four times that of student enrollment growth. These additional personnel were disproportionately non-teachers. While the number of FTE teachers increased almost two and a half times as fast as the increase in students—resulting in significantly smaller class sizes—the number of non-teachers or "all other staff" increased more than seven times the increase in students.

Despite this large investment in additional personnel, there does not seem to have been much return in terms of measured student outcomes. . . . [The staffing surge since 1992, when NAEP's main tests became available] has not led to measurable academic benefits for American public school students.

9. Mathematics and Reading Coaches Haven't Made a Significant Difference

Has the addition of math and reading coaches made a difference? In a thorough review of research in mathematics education in 2008, a group of nationally known scholars and researchers concluded as follows:

> In an attempt to improve mathematics learning at the elementary level, a number of school districts around the country are using "math specialist teachers" of three different types—math coaches (lead teachers), full-time elementary mathematics teachers, and pull-out teachers. However, the Panel found no high-quality research showing that the use of any of these types of math specialist teachers improves students' learning.[28] (p. xxii)

Apparently there has not been enough research on the effectiveness of reading coaches for conclusions to be drawn. About the best that a 2010 review could say in its conclusion was, "a positive and significant relationship between coached teachers and student achievement gains appear promising in initial research studies."[29]

10. Changes in Pedagogy in Reading and Mathematics Haven't Made a Difference

What about changes in pedagogy in reading and mathematics in the past three or four decades? First, we do not know if changes have been made on a large scale. And if there have, are the changes in the direction of the findings from high-quality research on beginning reading and arithmetic?[30]

If large-scale changes have been made, there is no evidence from National Assessment of Educational Progress (NAEP) tests or any of college admission tests in high school that low achievement has been addressed by them. So far as we can tell, we have percentage-wise at least as many low achievers (below Basic) in grade 12 in 2015 as we had in 1992, if not more.[31]

11. Standards Haven't (Overall) Made a Significant Difference

By the early 1990s, initially inspired by the standards issued in 1989 by the National Council for Teachers of Mathematics (NCTM), influential policy makers began to talk up the need for national standards in all major subjects.[32] Congress was not interested in national standards because they were and remain unconstitutional. However, states could legally develop their own standards (which would be optional for local school districts because of "local control").

But states could legally give statewide tests based on the standards their state boards of education had officially adopted. Their state departments of education could also issue sanctions for underperforming "schools" or districts.

Most state standards (from the 1980s on) did not accomplish what was chiefly intended by state standards—to equalize and upgrade what was taught in a state. Nor did any states make gaps between higher- and low-achieving groups disappear by grade 12, raising the question why policy makers in the USED or at the Gates Foundation in 2007/8 thought a common core of standards would improve low achievement. A recent analysis by the Brookings Institution confirms the high degree of skepticism the standards-based reform movement warrants.[33]

Even in Massachusetts, a state recognized as having academically strong standards and licensing requirements, and where all groups of students dramatically improved academically on NAEP tests after the late-1990s, the gaps had only slightly narrowed by 2010, to judge by NAEP scores. Most Bay State parents and teachers, so far as is known, were pleased that all groups of students were improving and were satisfied with the transparency of the state's standards-based tests. USED and the Gates Foundation were never interested in the reasons for the Bay State's effective standards, a lack of interest that has never been explained.

The idea that state standards would ensure equal and high expectations for all students in a state evolved as battles occurred in most states about who would write the standards, where would models come from, who would develop test items, who would review them, and who would set the cut (pass/fail) scores.[34] Only a few sets of pre-Common Core state standards have empirical evidence to support their value in increasing student achievement (Massachusetts in English, math, and science, and California in algebra I). No version of the Common Core-compliant standards in English language arts or mathematics that have been adopted by state boards of education in the past seven years has evidence to support its value today.

As Sandra Stotsky has tried to explain in a 2015 book, a state needs both academically strong teachers *and* academically strong K-12 standards to increase all students' academic achievement.[35] There is every reason to believe (as did Sputnik Era reformers) that textbooks/literature anthologies/curriculum objectives/lessons written or compiled by academic content experts are better in general than state standards in English language arts or mathematics.

12. Highly Academically Qualified Teachers Make a Difference But Are Getting Harder to Develop

Teachers are indeed a crucial factor in all students' education, but it is difficult to determine what a "high-quality teacher" is beyond someone who knows the subject matter they teach. The only characteristic of an effective teacher that turned up in the high-quality research examined by the National Mathematics Advisory Panel's task force on teacher education was teachers' knowledge of the subject(s) they teach or their verbal skills.[36] See chapter 6 for more details. Perhaps there have been changes in the academic quality of our teaching force that could account for a lack of progress by low (and higher) achievers?

A recent study compared the academic status of education majors (using, for example, their high school SAT/ACT scores) with peers in other subjects.[37] As Jonathan Wai reported, education majors consistently have the lowest academic aptitude on five independent tests from 1946 to 2014. He concluded, "These data show that US students who choose to major in education, essentially the bulk of people who become teachers, have for at least the last seven decades been selected from students at the lower end of the academic aptitude pool."

But a recent news report from Indiana is ominous. Thousands of prospective teachers are not passing licensure tests of the subject matter they plan to teach.[38] It is not clear if the problem lies in the new tests the state adopted, in the "cut" scores that Indiana teachers recommended, in the course of studies followed in college by these prospective teachers, in a lack of practice tests, or somewhere else.

The content of most teacher licensure tests of subject area knowledge is at the upper high school level of difficulty.[39] We also know that inflation of course grades has been a serious problem at the college level for several decades.[40] However, we don't know to what extent prospective teachers today have been the beneficiaries of new college programs that award academic credit for the college coursework they complete when it has been accompanied by courses described as "co-requisites" [41] or that enable students deemed "college and career ready" in grade 11 or 12 (on the basis of passing a Common Core-aligned test) to by-pass taking a college placement test that might indicate the need for a non-credit-bearing developmental course (a course below college level) in reading or mathematics.

It is too early to tell how many low achievers have been able to enroll in a four-year college program and complete a teacher preparation program with accumulated course credit from courses needing co-requisites and from courses that were once developmental courses. But there has been a concerted effort to eliminate placement tests and developmental courses in mathematics and reading in order to accelerate the college graduation rate for low achievers. The Race to the Top (RttT) applications asked states to commit to the elimination of remedial college-level courses and for a sign-off from officials at state institutions of higher learning.

For example, in Massachusetts, only a few state college mathematics instructors were invited to participate on a large higher education task force on mathematics charged with evaluating developmental courses and placement tests in mathematics at both community and state colleges. As a consequence of minimal participation by relevant faculty, the task force did not hear explanations of why such courses are needed and how useful they are to the students who take them. In an article published after the policy recommended by the task force was voted in by the Massachusetts Board of Higher Education, state college mathematics faculty members presented their explanations.[42] They pointed out that they could not even locate the minutes of the meetings held by the task force.

Nor were they able to explain at the board's meeting how misleading the references in the task force report were. None of the studies in the bibliography in its report provided evidence for the academic effectiveness of its recommendations for state colleges—to the effect that incoming students supposedly benefit mathematically from taking mathematics courses that are beyond their mathematical skill level.

Indeed, few studies listed in the annotated bibliography in the task force's report were even relevant to state colleges. The bibliography was skewed to community colleges and against the use of placement tests—a biased bibliography. But it is too early to tell how many low-achieving students in the Bay State—students who are no longer required to take placement tests at community or state colleges—will seek to become K-12 teachers, in particular Early Childhood or Elementary teachers.

KEY IDEAS TO REMEMBER

1. The nation's largest teacher organization suggests that low achievement can be attributed more to what schools, teachers, or parents have or have not done, or to their views of the student's competence, than to students' actual efforts or work habits.

2. The nation's largest teacher organization suggests that students are not responsible for their own academic learning.
3. Decades-long changes in the content of the reading/literature curriculum haven't enhanced student achievement.
4. Pre-school and home visiting programs, teacher professional development, and smaller classes have been generally ineffective in increasing student achievement or maintaining increases.
5. Making more instructional time available by means of longer school days or years has a mixed record and does not in itself improve low achievement.
6. Test-based retention seems useful but so far does not change the status of low achievers.
7. Full-service or community schools do not have a scaled-up record of effectiveness.
8. Decades-long increases in the ratio of non-teaching to teaching personnel (e.g., more mathematics and reading coaches) have not increased student achievement.
9. Changes in pedagogy in the last fifty years have not been shown to be effective in making low achievers higher achievers.
10. State or "national" standards and standards-based testing have yet to show they make a positive difference to most low achievers
11. Decline in teacher quality may have affected low achievers (as well as others).
12. So far, there is little or no evidence that massive low achievement is susceptible to educational interventions.

NOTES

1. "Identifying Factors that Contribute to Achievement Gaps, National Education Association," 2002-2017, http://www.nea.org/home/17413.htm.
2. "Basil Bernstein on Restricted and Elaborated Codes," n.d., http://neamathisi.com/new-learning/chapter-5-learning-personalities/basil-bernstein-on-restricted-and-elaborated-codes.
3. Tom Loveless, "Reading and math in the Common Core era," Brookings Institution, March 24, 2016,https://www.brookings.edu/research/reading-and-math-in-the-common-core-era/.
4. "The Current State of Scientific Knowledge on Pre-Kindergarten Effects," n.d., https://www.brookings.edu/wp-content/uploads/2017/04/duke_prekstudy_final_4-4-17_hires.pdf.
5. Karen R. Effrem, MD, "Government Preschools Don't Work. So Why Are We Still Funding Them?," *The National Pulse*, April 21, 2017, https://thenationalpulse.com/commentary/government-preschools-dont-work-taxpayers-funding/.
6. "2015-16 School and District Profiles: Boston Latin," http://profiles.doe.mass.edu/students/classsizebyraceethnicity.aspx?orgcode=00350560&fycode=2017&orgtypecode=6&.
7. Jason Sachs, "New P-2 Early Childhood Strategic Plan & Update on Boston Universal Preschool," April 26, 2017, https://www.bostonpublicschools.org/cms/lib/MA01906464/Centricity/Domain/162/Early%20Childhood%20Strategic%20Plan%

2020172022School%20Committee%20 presentation.pdf. For a different perspective on "diversity" at Boston Latin, see Ed Lyons, "There's no 'diversity problem' at Boston Latin," *New Boston Post*, June 25, 2016, http://newbostonpost.com/2016/06/25/theres-no-diversity-problem-at-boston-latin/.

8. "About Advanced Work Class Frequently Asked Questions," http://bostonpublicschools.org/cms/lib07/MA01906464/Centricity/Domain/216/awc_sy14_pamphlet_eng.pdf.

9. Lauren Camera, "The Effectiveness Dilemma:Teacher prep programs have mixed results but experts question President Donald Trump's decision to cut them." U.S. News, April 21, 2017,

10. Russell Gersten, Mary Jo Taylor, Tran D. Keys, Eric Rolfhus, and Rebecca Newman-Gonchar, *Summary of Research on the Effectiveness of Math Professional Development Approaches*, Regional Education Laboratory, 2014 (REL 2014–010), Washington, DC: U.S. Department of Education, Institute of Education Sciences, National Center for Education Evaluation and Regional Assistance, Regional Educational Laboratory Southeast, https://ies.ed.gov/ncee/edlabs/regions/southeast/pdf/REL_2014010.pdf.

11. National Mathematics Advisory Panel. *Foundations for Success: The Final Report of the National Mathematics Advisory Panel* (Washington, DC: U.S. Department of Education, 2008). https://www2.ed.gov/about/bdscomm/list/mathpanel/report/final-report.pdf.

12. Valerie F. Reyna, Chair, *Chapter 2: Report of the Subcommittee on Standards of Evidence*, National Mathematics Advisory Panel (Washington, DC: U.S. Department of Education, 2008), https://www2.ed.gov/about/bdscomm/list/mathpanel/report/standards-of-evidence.pdf.

13. Deborah Loewenberg Ball, Chair, *Chapter 5: Report of the Task Group on Teachers and Teacher Education*, National Mathematics Advisory Panel (Washington, DC: U.S. Department of Education, 2008), 5-40, https://www2.ed.gov/about/bdscomm/list/mathpanel/report/teachers.pdf.

14. Linda Darling-Hammond , Maria E. Hyler , and Madelyn Gardner , "Effective Teacher Professional Development," *Learning Policy Institute*, June 5, 2017, https://learningpolicyinstitute.org/product/effective-teacher-professional-development-report.

15. "The Gates Foundation Examines What Teachers Want in Professional Development ," Association of American Educators, March 13, 2015, https://www.aaeteachers.org/index.php/blog/1455-the-gates-foundation-examines-what-teachers-want-in-professional-development .

16. Lauren Camera, "Democrats Protest Cuts to Teacher Prep and Pell Grants," *U.S. News*, July 19, 2017, https://www.usnews.com/news/education-news/articles/2017-07-19/hundreds-of-house-democrats-protest-cuts-to-teacher-prep-and-pell-grants.

17. "Home Visiting Evidence of Effectiveness Review: Executive Summary," Department of Health and Human Services, April 2017, https://homvee.acf.hhs.gov/HomVEE_Executive_Summary_Summary_03162017.pdf.

18. Karen R. Effrem, MD, "President Trump, It's Time to End Home Visiting Programs," The National Pulse, April 14, 2017, https://thenationalpulse.com/commentary/president-trump-end-home-visiting-programs/ .

19. Barbara Nye, Larry V. Hedges, and Spyros Konstantopoulos, "Do Low-Achieving Students Benefit More from Small Classes? Evidence from the Tennessee Class Size Experiment," *Educational Evaluation and Policy Analysis*, September 1, 2002, http://journals.sagepub.com/doi/abs/10.3102/01623737024003201.

20. Tim Walker, "A 9 to 5 School Day: Are Longer Hours Better for Students and Educators?" *neaToday*, November 22, 2016, http://neatoday.org/2016/11/22/longer-school-days/; "Expanded Learning Time: A Summary of Findings from Case Studies in Four States," Center on Education Policy, January 2015, http://files.eric.ed.gov/fulltext/ED555412.pdf.

21. "10 Telling Studies Done on Longer School Days," *Online Universities*, January 30, 2012, http://www.onlineuniversities.com/10-telling-studies-done-on-longer-school-days.

22. Stacey Joyner and Concepcion Molina,"Class Time and Student Learning," Texas Comprehensive Center, January 2012, http://www.sedl.org/txcc/resources/briefs/number6/.

23. Michael Hansen and Diana Quintero, "Analyzing 'the homework gap' among high school students," Brookings Institution, August 10, 2017, https://www.brookings.edu/blog/brown-center-chalkboard/2017/08/10/analyzing-the-homework-gap-among-high-school-students/.

24. G. Schwerdt and M.R. West, "The Effects of Test-based Retention on Student Outcomes over Time: Regression Discontinuity Evidence from Florida." Program on Education Policy and Governance, Working Papers Series, Harvard Kennedy School, February 2013. https://www.hks.harvard.edu/pepg/PDF/Papers/PEPG12-09_West.pdf.

25. https://learningpolicyinstitute.org/product/community-schools-equitable-improvement-brief.

26. Will Dobbie and Roland G. Fryer Jr., "Are High-Quality Schools Enough to Increase Achievement among the Poor? Evidence from the Harlem Children's Zone," *American Economic Journal: Applied Economics*, Vol.3, No. 3, July 2011, 158-87, http://www.aeaweb.org/articles.php?doi=10.1257/app.3.3.158.

27. Benjamin Scafidi, "Back to the Staffing Surge," EdChoice, Indianapolis, May 2017, https://www.edchoice.org/wp-content/uploads/2017/05/Back-to-the-Staffing-Surge-by-Ben-Scafidi.pdf.

28. Ibid.

29. "A Study of the Effectiveness of K–3 Literacy Coaches," NRTAC, 2010, 37, https://www2.ed.gov/programs/readingfirst/support/effectivenessfinal.pdf; Jennifer Sloan McCombs and Julie A. Marsh "Lessons for Boosting the Effectiveness of Reading Coaches," *Sage Journals*, March 1, 2009, http://journals.sagepub.com/doi/abs/10.1177/0031721709090000710?journalCode=pdka.

30. "Teaching reading: whole language and phonics," Wikipedia, n.d., https://en.wikipedia.org/wiki/Teaching_reading:_whole_language_and_phonics ; and National Mathematics Advisory Panel. *Foundations for Success: The Final Report of the National Mathematics Advisory Panel* (Washington, D.C.: U.S. Department of Education, 2008), https://www2.ed.gov/about/bdscomm/list/mathpanel/report/final-report.pdf.

31. The Nation's Report Card, "2015 | Mathematics & Reading at Grade 12,"

32. "High Standards for All Students," October 1994, https://www2.ed.gov/pubs/studstnd.html.

33. Tom Loveless, "Predicting the Effect of Common Core State Standards on Student Achievement," Brookings Institution, February 2012, https://www.brookings.edu/wp-content/uploads/2016/06/0216_brown_education_loveless.pdf; and Valerie Strauss, "Common Core Won't Likely Boost Student Achievement, Analysis Says," *Washington Post*, February 18, 2012, https://www.washingtonpost.com/blogs/answer-sheet/post/common-core-wont-likely-boost-student-achievement-analysis-says/2012/02/16/gIQAOfZuJR_blog.html?utm_term=.dcac18dfbb41.

34. Sandra Stotsky, editor, *What's at Stake in the K-12 Standards Wars: A Primer for Educational Policy Makers,* 3rd Edition, https://www.amazon.com/Whats-Stake-K-12-Standards-Wars/dp/0820444901.

35. Sandra Stotsky, *An Empty Curriculum: The Need to Reform Teacher Licensing Regulations and Tests*, https://www.amazon.com/Empty-Curriculum-Teacher-Licensing-Regulations/dp/1475815662.

36. Ibid.

37. Jonathan Wai, "Your college major is a pretty good indication of how smart you are." *Quartz Media LLC (US)*. February 3, 2015, https://qz.com/334926/your-college-major-is-a-pretty-good-indication-of-how-smart-you-are/.

38. Bob Segall, "Crisis in the classroom: New Indiana teachers repeatedly failing state exam," WTHR, March 7, 2017, http://www.wthr.com/article/crisis-in-the-classroom-new-indiana-teachers-repeatedly-failing-state-exams.

39. See, for example, Ruth Mitchell and Patte Barthe. "How Teacher Licensing Tests Fall Short," *Thinking K-16*, 1999, 3(1), 3-23; also Ruth Mitchell and Patte Barthe, *Not Good Enough: A Content Analysis of Teacher Licensing Exams*, a report issued by Education Trust in Summer 1999, https://eric.ed.gov/?id=ED457261.

40. For example, see Catherine Rampell, "A History of College Grade Inflation," *New York Times*, July 14, 2011, https://economix.blogs.nytimes.com/2011/07/14/the-history-of-college-grade-inflation/?hp.

41. For example, see Bruce Vandal, "Corequisites and Closing Opportunity Gaps," *Complete College America*, June 11, 2014, http://completecollege.org/corequisites-and-closing-opportunity-gaps/ ; and Joseph Williams, "Colleges Remake Remedial Education by Going Back to High School," *EdSurge*, February 20, 2017, https://www.edsurge.com/news/2017-02-20-colleges-remake-remedial-education-by-going-back-to-high-school.

42. Mike Winders and Richard Bisk, "Math Task Force's Bad Calculation," *New England Journal of Higher Education*, September 30, 2014, http://www.nebhe.org/thejournal/math-task-forces-bad-calculation/.

SIX

Who Should Teach Low-Achieving Students—and All the Others?

This chapter addresses issues in defining and ensuring teacher quality. It focuses on teachers because they turned out to be the most important school-based factor in the 1966 Coleman Report, still considered a major reference for understanding the problems this country faces in achieving "equality of educational opportunity," the title of the report. The major issue today is which trumps the other: teacher diversity or teacher quality.

In the context of the many failed strategies and approaches to which one can point in the fifty-year attempt to raise the achievement of low-achieving students, "teacher quality" needs more attention. However it is defined, it is considered the major factor related to student achievement, positively or negatively.

WHAT IS TEACHER QUALITY?

But what exactly "teacher quality" is—what student achievement is actually related to—depends on a researcher's idiosyncratic definition of the phrase. Does it refer to teachers: with a high school diploma (and if so, one based on a General Education Diploma [GED] or on three to four-years of high school attendance); with a high grade point average (GPA) in high school; with high SAT or ACT scores before or after alignment with Common Core's standards; or with specific college majors?

Does teacher quality refer to someone with a certain number and kind of college courses taken in the arts and sciences; with a certain number and kind of education courses taken in a teacher preparation program; with passing scores on licensure tests of subject area knowledge and on how the quality of the test is judged; with certification or licensure in a discipline-based field; with an undergraduate degree (and if so, from an education school or a non-education school); or with graduate degrees (master's or doctoral), and if so, from an education school or a non-education school? There are differences in the academic and pedagogical competencies a teacher is likely to have, depending on each of these variables.

That is why much rides on the researcher's definition of "teacher quality." Research on teacher quality is meaningless if teacher quality doesn't include some measures of a teacher's academic background (not effectiveness per se, or students' test scores) and if researchers don't clarify exactly what they mean by the phrase.

WHAT IS THE ACADEMIC QUALITY OF THE TEACHING FORCE?

The intense focus on low achievers since 1965 may have already led teacher education in the United States in the wrong direction. This country likely has more low achievers as teachers already teaching than any other industrialized country would tolerate. That means teachers who learned little in high school, took minimally demanding undergraduate courses, and/or accumulated academic credits toward a college degree based on coursework with little academic content.

A 2010 McKinsey report provided information on the relatively low academic background of most teachers in the United States.[1] Its title gives the punch line away: *Closing the Talent Gap: Attracting and Retaining Top-Third Graduates to Careers in Teaching*. As the report noted, most of the teaching force in the United States comes from the bottom third of its college cohort. And, to judge from the numbers in Massachusetts who take licensure tests,[2] many academically low-achieving teachers are likely in Early Childhood or Elementary teacher programs, the two programs with the largest number of prospective teachers (the case in most states). These teachers are responsible for laying the foundations for every major subject that students study in grades K–12.

These grim findings have been confirmed in other reports. Using as indices five different tests that have been given over the past half century, Jonathan Wai reported enormous differences in academic aptitude between undergraduates who major in education in the United States and those with other undergraduate majors; education majors consistently have the lowest academic aptitude on five independent tests from 1946 to 2014.[3] Education majors don't necessarily have the lowest grade point averages in college—in part because of the grading criteria used for education coursework.[4]

In contrast, Finland draws all its pre-college teachers from the top 20 percent or so of those who graduate from its academic high schools (grades ten to twelve)—public schools that enroll less than 50 percent of its school-age cohort after compulsory education ends in grade nine. In an intensely competitive environment, Finland admits only a small number to its lengthy teacher preparation programs (five years for prospective elementary teachers).

Moreover, Finland's many teacher preparation programs were reduced in number in its earliest education reforms in 1970, and the eight survivors were/are located at its universities. Not surprisingly, Pasi Sahlberg, a well-known Finnish educator, has little to say about the content of professional development for Finnish teachers in *Finnish Lessons*, his 2011 book.[5]

Do current American policy makers believe that a teacher who was a low-achieving high school or college student can better empathize with a low-achieving K–12 student and inspire that student to read and study more? We don't know. Researchers haven't distinguished among *today's* K–12 teachers with respect to their academic backgrounds and compared their effects on their students. Nor is there research on whether effective teaching of low achievers is related to the extent of empathy in whatever low-achieving teachers they had. Researchers seem to be pre-occupied with teachers' and students' ethnic and racial backgrounds.

Much of what we can find out about reading and mathematics achievement is in the nation's "Report Cards" at three grade levels and ages. We can find out, for example, that from 1992 to 2015 the percentage of children below Basic in reading in grade four declined from 38 percent to 31 percent—a movement in the right direction.[6] But NAEP or the National Center for Education Statistics (NCES) seems to offer little if anything on the reading teachers of these low-achievers.

Nor is there any research showing that teachers who were low achievers can effectively teach the range of students their license legally allows them to teach. Why does this matter? It matters because a licensed teacher who was a low achiever and who has been judged in some way to teach low-achieving students effectively cannot legally be constrained to teach only low-achieving students. A teaching license means the holder can teach the full range of children designated by the grade span in the license.

Once a teacher is licensed, she can legally teach high- or higher-performing students as well as low-achieving students at the grade levels or for the subjects designated by the license. There is no research on the results of using teachers of any ethnicity or race who had been low achievers in contrast to teachers of any ethnicity or race who had been high-achievers to teach high- or higher-performing students of any ethnicity or race.

It is understandable why federal, state, and local education policy makers may have concluded that academically weak teachers need to know more about the subject they teach and/or the pedagogy for teaching those subjects. It is not understandable why they have not also logically concluded that academically weak high school or college students should *not* be admitted to teacher preparation programs, to begin with.

THE MAJOR OBSTACLE IN STRENGTHENING TEACHER QUALITY

State and national education policy makers and legislators have already shown a lack of logic in their willingness to reauthorize and refund programs that failed to educate low-achieving students. And in their failure to insist upon sunset clauses and rigorous evaluations of the programs they do fund. Thus, it is not surprising that attempts to strengthen admission criteria for teacher preparation programs have run into many buzz saws.

Probably the biggest buzz saw is concern for the "cash cow"—the tuition money that the typically large number of college students in teacher preparation programs, especially early childhood or elementary programs, bring in, together with the marginally extra costs of preparing them for a career in teaching.[7] If the cash cow is viewed as people who love children and have always wanted to be teachers, how can low academic competence matter?

ORIGINS AND EVOLUTION OF TEACHER QUALITY CONTROLS

Even teacher licensure tests (tests designed to protect students from academically incompetent teachers) are called "obstacles" by economists and others.[8] Yet they have been used for centuries in Europe and this country. Few policy makers or researchers know much about them.

Their origins were the examinations used to certify teachers at European church-sponsored universities. In this country's earliest days, potential teachers of a community's children needed to convince local ministers of their moral character, soundness of faith, as well as academic accomplishments.

As public schooling expanded, especially after compulsory education was initiated in Massachusetts in 1852, teacher examinations spread throughout the country. They expanded to the state level once states entered the Union, although cities and counties often retained their own examinations, typically focused on a candidate's moral character and knowledge of common school subjects.

A considerable amount of content knowledge (and, correspondingly, little pedagogical knowledge) was assessed on these examinations, as suggested by an investigation of the teacher tests given in nineteenth-century Wisconsin and California and turn-of-the-twentieth century Michigan by Richard Askey, a mathematician at the University of Wisconsin.[9] It is worth looking at what was required then.

The credits for the twenty topics on the March 1875 exam in nineteenth-century California totaled one thousand. The grade levels for which a license would be valid depended on getting a certain number of credits in key areas (Written Grammar and Spelling). Rote memorization was clearly not expected by most test questions. Askey gives the following examples of history questions on an exam in 1900 for candidates who wanted to teach in a grammar school in Michigan:

- Tell what work was accomplished by Miltiades, and state its effect upon the country.
- Briefly describe Ireland during the reign of Elizabeth.
- Briefly state the result and effect of the battle of Waterloo, naming the leading general.
- What was the bone of contention between Austria and Germany in 1866?
- Give the result and effect of this trouble.
- Name the leaders of the Italian struggle for freedom, and state the result of their efforts.
- Mention some supplementary reading which you would recommend in a history class.
- When was the present form of government in France organized, and who is president today?

Keep in mind that candidates did not have to be more than high school graduates then. Today, it is unlikely that a college graduate aiming for a "middle school" license today could answer similar essay questions.

Certification by examination was eventually supplanted by the acceptance of credentials showing completion of a prescribed sequence of school or college courses as college and normal school training programs expanded in the second half of the nineteenth century and the early decades of the twentieth. Although mandatory examinations declined in the early twentieth century, they continued in many large cities largely because of the demand for urban teaching positions. In rural areas, examinations were used to grant "emergency" licenses to candidates who had not completed professional training.

Despite some criticism of the quality of teacher examinations years ago, their use was considered unavoidable. Training institutions did not graduate enough candidates to fill the growing number of teaching positions available. Locally made examinations could assure a community of a minimal level of a teacher's academic competence, a legal possibility for any community even today, since it would not be a license that only a state agency can award but a locally required supplement to a state license.

Thus, given the important role of the teacher in student achievement, it is surprising that in offering summary advice on how to "transform" low-achieving schools, the federal government makes no useful recommendations on how to strengthen academically low achievers' teachers.[10] In fact, many of the recommended strategies offered in a 1998 document for "turning around" low-performing schools are not supported by a clear and agreed-upon body of evidence (e.g., from studies on professional development for teachers, extended learning time for students). No suggestions address the issues highlighted by research on the use of these supposedly effective "strategies."

Today, we seem to have a new set of buzz words to designate an elusive "teacher quality." High-performing schools have been described as "high quality" simply or chiefly by virtue of their test results. Educators are expected to pay attention to a fine-sounding phrase "excellence in teaching and leadership." What exactly "excellence in teaching" looks like is difficult to grasp, however. According to a report on "strategies to improve low-performing schools" issued by the Center for American Progress in 2016, the phrase seems to designate a key factor supposedly found in high-performing charter schools.[11]

The phrase has been used by Roland Fryer, a prominent Harvard economist known for his attempt to inject seemingly successful charter school practices into "traditional" schools. According to the center's 2016 report, the vast school improvement program he helped to design in 2010 for Houston, Texas, "implemented the following best practices of high-performing charters" based on Fryer's research on effective schooling models: (1) data-driven instruction; (2) excellence in teaching and leadership; (3) a culture of high expectations; (4) frequent and intensive tutoring, or so-called high-dosage tutoring; and (5) an extended school day and year.

The results of Houston's Apollo program have been described as "statistically significant" gains in mathematics but "negligible" gains in reading. Moreover, "high-dosage tutoring" seemed to be the source of the mathematics gains. For Fryer's account of the Houston program and its results, see his 2013 article.[12] For other accounts of the program and its results, see the October 2013 article by a *Houston Press* reporter,[13] the February 2014 evaluation of the Houston program by Rice University, as well as a reporter's account of the evaluation,[14] a February 2014 article by a *Houston Chronicle* reporter,[15] and a December 2014 article by the *Houston Press* reporter, now its editor in chief.[16]

So what does "excellence in teaching" seem to designate? According to the center's 2016 report, it means "teachers who are resilient, hardworking, and dedicated, and also able to work with diverse populations, have a thorough understanding of high-quality instruction, and maintain high expectations for students." Hiring practices used by high-performing charter schools "include screening applicants for their resilience, work ethic, high expectations for students, effect on student learning, past achievement, and leadership."

If anything, excellence in teaching low achievers seems to mean that the students get higher test scores. We do not know if that is what it means to most school administrators today, whether their students are low or higher achievers.

Fryer has claimed that there is little relationship between student scores in high-performing charter schools and "the fraction of teachers with teaching certification, and the fraction of teachers with an advanced degree."[17] What that seems to mean is that teaching excellence is *not* related to the teacher's possession of a teaching license or an advanced degree.

Fryer does not explain why a teaching license *should necessarily have ever meant* that the teacher is a better teacher. Many private schools — sectarian or nonsectarian — do not have to hire licensed teachers, and many traditionally have avoided hiring state-licensed teachers. Nor does he explain what he means by an "advanced degree." If it means or includes an MEd, there was never any reason to infer that its holder knows more about anything (including pedagogy) than someone without an MEd. Perhaps Fryer is simply speaking as economists do these days; they tend to see teacher licensure tests as "obstacles." Maybe "advanced degrees," too.

The Houston results leave policy makers with a conundrum. Low achievers seemed to respond to intensive math tutorials (all Houston students had regular math classes; only some had tutorials too). On the other hand, it isn't clear that targeted and intensive tutoring can achieve more than immediate higher test results (i.e., lasting gains) and in both reading and math. Rice University's evaluation recommended not only more math tutorials but also tutorials in reading for the future. What do the seeming effectiveness of math tutorials in Houston and a recommendation for reading tutorials tell education schools (which typically do not prepare teachers to do tutorials)?

QUALITY OF UNDERGRADUATE TEACHER PREPARATION PROGRAMS

For sixty years, the academic demands of prospective teachers' undergraduate education in the Arts and Sciences have been declining.[18] At the same time that academic or content courses were declining in demand, the requirements of undergraduate (or post-baccalaureate) programs for teacher preparation (usually in an education school) were increasing to address the various social, cultural, and linguistic issues that education faculty saw as necessary for pre-service teachers.

These new requirements have resulted in a typical training program whose content Arthur Levine described as "unruly and chaotic" in *Educating School Teachers* — a highly critical report on teacher education released in 2006.[19] After visiting or conducting surveys in hundreds of institutions across the country, the former president of Teachers College, Columbia University, and his research staff concluded that most teacher training programs suffered from low standards, out-of-touch faculty, and poor quality control.

Among Levine's recommendations was the suggestion that this country needed to reduce the number of teacher preparation programs to those located at universities where the qualifications for admission were the most demanding.[20] This idea is similar to what Finnish reformers did in the 1970s when they first began education reform in Finland.

Most, if not all, of the recommendations in Levine's report (funded chiefly by the Annenberg, Ford, and Kauffman Foundations) have been studiously ignored since it was issued. The nation's colleges seem to want to enroll as many low-achieving students as they can entice. And with federal largesse, one suspects they will consider providing formal mentoring programs to help them to pass their courses when there is more evidence.[21]

Few policy makers, college officials, or legislators overtly want to keep low-achieving college students from becoming teachers, although they do make sure through pamphlets on the topic that low-achieving college students understand what they need to do to become teachers.[22] But there are no monetary incentives in school salary scales or elsewhere to hint that an Arts and Sciences major in a subject taught in K–12 is more desirable for any prospective secondary school teacher than other kinds of majors, or to reward the practicing teacher who seeks an MA or MS in the Arts and Sciences instead of a MEd.

DIVERSITY OR QUALITY IN K–12 TEACHERS

Although most rational people in this country want academically competent teachers in the classroom, there is a dilemma. Illinois may be the first state to confront the dilemma. Many students failed a new test in Illinois required before admission to a teacher preparation program (called Test of Academic Proficiency or TAP[23]), and many of those failing the test were black and Hispanic.[24] Instead of calling those who failed the test "low scorers," they were called "minorities" or black and Hispanic.

The dilemma stems from calling students who fail a teacher-licensing test black or Hispanic rather than simply low scorers. The issue in Illinois became not why students admitted to a public college failed a basic skills test but the quality of the test and the cut (pass/fail) score to be set, enabling the right proportion of blacks or Hispanics to be eligible for admission to a teacher preparation program. No one in a "leadership" position suggested letting parents have a say about this.

K–12 schools want and need teachers from any demographic background. But most are unlikely to want to hire teachers who couldn't pass a basic skills test—to teach either their low- or higher-achieving students. If prospective teachers who fail a licensure test are identified as black or minority, then policy makers, legislators, or school administrators trying to raise academic achievement are accused of bigotry in opposing the hiring of low-scoring teachers. As is known, the only characteristic of effective teachers found in high-quality research is mastery of the subject(s) they teach.[25]

If a case is also made that diversity is reduced by keeping out test takers who have failed a licensure test designed to protect the students of future K–12 teachers, then those making the case have related diversity to low achievement and unmoored teacher licensure from its traditional role of protecting students and their parents. If pursuit of diversity in a teaching staff requires hiring teachers who would have failed their licensure tests or who couldn't be described with at least several of the academic descriptors of teacher quality listed at the beginning of this chapter, then the pursuit of diversity in a teaching staff becomes anti-educational.

A test taker who scores low on a basic skills licensure test is unlikely to be an effective teacher of any subject or group of students. Equating failure to pass a licensure test with reduction of diversity degrades the concept of diversity.

By allowing the substitution of other measures (such as their high school SAT or ACT score) to enable otherwise low scorers on a basic skills test to get into public teacher preparation programs, Illinois policy makers temporarily disguised the basic problem in Illinois but did not solve it. It is no longer clear what the scores on the SAT or the ACT now mean after both tests were "aligned" to Common Core's standards—controversial and vague K–12 standards in reading/English language arts and mathematics.

The consequences of having to admit students into teacher preparation programs who might have been low scorers on a test of basic skills but who have chosen to submit high school scores that are now uninterpretable fall on the faculty in the education school and in the public school where student teaching occurs. The consequences no longer fall just on the school personnel that once hired these prospective teachers after they had passed measures based on the lower standards in place earlier.

Now school and education school faculty must figure out how to pass low-scoring and low-performing student teachers (or student teachers with uninterpretable SAT or ACT scores) in their coursework and in their student teaching. Otherwise, the faculty and cooperating teachers themselves will be accused of bigotry (unless the student teachers were higher-achieving students in disguise).

Needless to say, the chief and first victims of low performers in teacher preparation programs are all the K–12 students in the student teacher's classroom. Nothing legally prevents them from student-teaching the full range of young students in subjects or at grade levels covered by the license they seek, even though such student teachers are unlikely to be able to teach any subject effectively.

The bandwagon is already rolling. Licensing teachers is being declared tantamount to excluding "teachers of color."[26] It is even being implied that licensing was part of Jim Crow. *Chalkbeat*'s reporter Matt Barnum asserts, erroneously, "The modern incarnation of teacher competency tests began in the South in the 1970s, coinciding with extensive court efforts to integrate schools, and spread quickly; critics at the time said their purpose was to exclude black teachers."

Barnum also got the purpose for licensure wrong. "The goal of the certification tests and rules is to screen out teachers who aren't likely to succeed on the job." What can black and Hispanic parents do when they're not even asked by the media what they most want in their children's math teacher: knowledge of the math to be taught at their grade level (and several above or below that) or matching skin color and ethnicity.

SPEAKING UP FOR QUALITY FIRST

Ensuring that diversity means academic quality in a teaching force requires speaking up. The best example comes from a member of the Massachusetts Board of Education when it was faced with approving a pass/fail score for a new elementary mathematics licensure test that meant that only 27 percent of the test takers (prospective teachers of children from birth to grade six) would pass.

The official minutes of the May 19, 2009, meeting containing the paragraph below don't capture the tension (or the exact words spoken) at this point in the meeting. The discussion then was about the effect on diversity of a recommended pass score that amounted to getting 60 percent of the items correct on a forty-item test of elementary mathematics.

The test had been developed and vetted by the state's own mathematics educators and mathematicians. The state's mathematics organizations were all in favor of the test as well as the recommended cut score.[27] No one in these organizations testified against the test or recommended cut score, but one board member tried to raise an argument against them.

> Vice Chair Chernow said her concern is that teacher licensing is already overly complex and bureaucratic, and additional tests complicate it further. She said that 46 states use the Praxis test, and asked whether using a different test [the new test] impedes reciprocity and teacher mobility. Dr. Howard said he appreciated the expressions of concern

about the diversity of the teaching pool, but standards should be set based on what students require from their teachers. Dr. Stotsky said the Praxis test [for elementary teachers] is weak on mathematics. (6–7)

Dr. Howard, whose undergraduate and graduate degrees were both from Harvard University, said something in my recollection of the discussion closer to "Quality comes first. Then look for diversity."[28] He is an African American, and there was no further discussion of this issue by the board. The recommended cut score and test were approved unanimously. About 50 percent of the test takers across test administrations on average have passed the test since the board's decision. No information is available on race or ethnicity.

CONCLUDING REMARKS

A major question in Illinois or in any other state today is why parents can't contribute to the decision on where the pass schore should be for children's teachers. Why can an education school professor threaten a teacher shortage in Illinois if low scorers aren't able to get licensed? And his is not the only one threatening a teacher shortage based on self-interest. A well-funded organization trying to influence the public purse is also saber-rattling, while a research organization tries to get the facts out to the public.

This conversation lacks parents' perspectives. What might parents' priorities be in a teacher for their own children—a match of race/ethnicity or clear evidence of the teacher's academic competence? Why are non-parents making the decision for parents?

As Dan Goldhaber noted in his article in the Spring 2016 issue of *Education Next*, "[O]f the characteristics [of teacher quality] that were measured in the still-revered 1966 Coleman report titled 'Equality of Educational Opportunity,' those that bear the highest relationship to pupil achievement are first, the teacher's score on the verbal skill test, and then his educational background." The differential importance of a teacher's verbal skills in student achievement is confirmed by the findings of a study of the relationship between students' academic achievement and the scores of white, Hispanic, and black teachers in a Texas school district on a test of prospective teachers' skills.

Why, all parents might ask, shouldn't all teachers be expected to have high verbal skills on tests of these skills, as well as a strong academic background? Why should some parents get low-scoring teachers for their children as a matter of public policy? Why should diversity in a school's teaching staff depend on some teachers having low or uninterpretable scores on basic tests of academic competence?

KEY IDEAS TO REMEMBER

1. Teacher quality should include a prospective or practicing teacher's academic background, however else it is defined.
2. No research shows that American teachers who were low achievers can teach higher-achieving students effectively.
3. A licensed teacher can be hired to teach any grades or subjects covered by the license.
4. Education schools have long used the excessive number of prospective teachers in their Early Childhood and Elementary School preparation programs as "cash cows."
5. Teacher licensure tests, beginning in Europe centuries ago, were designed to protect students from academically incompetent teachers.
6. The curriculum in most education schools has been described as "unruly and chaotic."
7. Today, public schools need academically strong teachers.
8. Parents have not been asked by policy makers if they prefer teachers who know the subject matter they are licensed to teach or matching race/ethnicity.

NOTES

1. Byron Auguste, Paul Kihn, and Matt Miller, *Closing the Talent Gap: Attracting and Retaining Top-Third Graduates to Careers in Teaching*, (Washington, DC: McKinsey and Company, September 2010), 23, http://www.teindia.nic.in/files/articles/closing_the_talent_gap.pdf.

2. "Massachusetts Tests for Educator Licensure (MTEL), Past Test Administrations," http://www.doe.mass.edu/mtel/results.html.

3. Jonathan Wai, "Your College Major Is a Pretty Good Indication of How Smart You Are," *Quartz Media*, February 3, 2015, https://qz.com/334926/your-college-major-is-a-pretty-good-indication-of-how-smart-you-are/.

4. C. Koedel, "Grade Inflation for Education Majors and Low Standards For Teachers" (Washington, DC: American Enterprise Institute, August 22, 2011), https://www.aei.org/publication/grade-inflation-for-education-majors-and-low-standards-for-teachers/.

5. Sandra Stotsky, "The Serpent in Finland's Garden of Equity: Essay Review of *Finnish Lessons: What Can the World Learn from Educational Change in Finland* by Pasi Sahlberg (New York: Teachers College Press, 2011)," Pioneer Institute, February 1, 2012, http://pioneerinstitute.org/wp-content/uploads/dlm_uploads/Finland_Stotsky.pdf.

6. NCES, *The Condition of Education 2017*, chapter 3, "Figure 1: Average NAEP Scale Scores of 4th, 8th, and 12th Grade Students, 1992–2015," https://nces.ed.gov/programs/coe/pdf/coe_cnb.pdf. While the direction is right, how can a nation survive with one-third of its children unable to read at a grade-four level by the age of nine or ten?

7. Stephen Dinham, "Standards Will Slide while Teacher Education Is Used as a Cash Cow," *The Conversation* , January 17, 2013, http://theconversation.com/standards-will-slide-while-teacher-education-is-used-as-a-cash-cow-11677.

8. Sandra Stotsky, *An Empty Curriculum: The Need to Reform Teacher Licensing Regulations and Tests* (Lanham, MD: Rowman & Littlefield, 2015), chap. 10.

9. Richard Askey, "Examinations for Teachers in the Past and Present," *Schoolinfosystem*, http://www.schoolinfosystem.org/pdf/2007/04/askeymadlit.pdf.

10. "Focus on Learning: Promising Strategies for Improving Student Achievement," Turning Around Low-Performing Schools: A Guide for State and Local Leaders," May 1998, https://www2.ed.gov/pubs/turning/strategy.html.

11. Chelsea Straus and Tiffany D. Miller, "Strategies to Improve Low-Performing Schools under the Every Student Succeeds Act: How 3 Districts Found Success Using Evidence-Based Practices," Center for American Progress, March 2, 2016, https://www.americanprogress.org/issues/education/reports/2016/03/02/132053/strategies-to-improve-low-performing-schools-under-the-every-student-succeeds-act/.

12. Roland G. Fryer Jr., "Injecting Successful Charter School Strategies into Traditional Public Schools: A Field Experiment in Houston," NBER Working Paper No. 1749, revised December 12, 2013, http://www.nber.org/papers/w17494.

13. Margaret Downing, "Apollo 20 Figures Out How to Improve Math Scores, but Reading Remains an Unsolved Equation," *Houston Press*, October 24, 2013, http://www.houstonpress.com/news/apollo-20-figures-out-how-to-improve-math-scores-but-reading-remains-an-unsolved-equation-6744069.

14. Ruth N. López Turley, "Review of Dr. Roland Fryer's Apollo 20 Report—Injecting Charter School Best Practices into Traditional Public Schools: Evidence from Houston," *Research Brief*, February 2014, https://kinder.rice.edu/uploadedFiles/Kinder_Institute_for_Urban_Research/Programs/HERC/Apollo%2020.pdf; see also Amy McCaig, "HISD's Apollo 20 Program Should Expand Tutoring, according to Rice Review," *Rice University News and Media*, February 12, 2014, http://news.rice.edu/2014/02/12/hisds-apollo-20-program-should-expand-tutoring-according-to-rice-review-2/.

15. Allan Turner, "Review Questions Staying Power of Gains in HISD Apollo Program," Houston Chronicle, February 12, 2014, http://www.houstonchronicle.com/news/houston-texas/houston/article/Review-questions-staying-power-of-gains-in-HISD-5229488.php.

16. Margaret Downing, "Rewriting History: Apollo 20's Legacy as It Is Now, Was Once and What It Was Supposed to Be," *Houston Press*, December 2, 2014, http://www.houstonpress.com/news/rewriting-history-apollo-20s-legacy-as-it-is-now-was-once-and-what-it-was-supposed-to-be-6735683.

17. National Review Online, "Lessons from New York City's Most Effective Charter Schools," ExcelinEd, January 7, 2014, http://www.excelined.org/news/lessons-new-york-citys-effective-charter-schools/.

18. Sandra Stotsky, "The Case for Broadening Veteran Teachers' Education in the Liberal Arts and How We Can Do It," in *Beyond the Basics: Achieving a Liberal Education for All Children*, ed. Chester Finn and Diane Ravitch (Washington DC: Thomas B. Fordham Institute, 2007), 95–107, http://www.edexcellencemedia.net/publications/2007/200707_beyondthebasics/Beyond_The_Basics_Stotsky.pdf.

19. Arthur Levine, *Educating School Teachers* (Washington, DC: The Education Schools Project., 2006), http://edschools.org/pdf/Educating_Teachers_Report.pdf.

20. See especially Levine's "Recommendation Five," in *Educating School Teachers*, 111.

21. Geri Salinitri, "The Effects of Formal Mentoring on the Retention Rates for First-Year, Low Achieving Students," *Canadian Journal of Education / Revue canadienne de l'éducation* 28, no. 4 (2005): 853–73, http://www.jstor.org/stable/4126458?seq=1#page_scan_tab_contents.

22. See, for example, St. Francis College of Education, "Illinois PEL—Basic Skills Test Requirement," https://www.stfrancis.edu/ilpel-basic-skills/.

23. For a description of the test, see "Test of Academic Proficiency (TAP) (400)," Illinois Licensure Testing System, https://www.il.nesinc.com/TestView.aspx?f=HTML_FRAG/IL400_TestPage.html. For current pass rates, see "Illinois Licensure Testing System Best Attempt Pass Rate by Test of Academic Proficiency Subtest, January 1, 2017 and March 31, 2017," https://www.isbe.net/Documents/TAP_PassRates400_20170101_20170331.pdf.

24. Odette Yousef, "Push for Teacher Quality in Illinois Takes Toll on Minority Candidates," WBEZ, September 4, 2013, https://www.wbez.org/shows/wbez-news/push-for-teacher-quality-in-illinois-takes-toll-on-minority-candidates/4424e1cd-6d87-480d-99f4-8e374fc36741.

25. Deborah Loewenberg Ball, *Report of the Task Group on Teachers and Teacher Education* (Washington, DC: National Mathematics Advisory Panel, 2008), 5–21, https://www2.ed.gov/about/bdscomm/list/mathpanel/report/teachers.pdf.

26. Matt Barnum, "Certification Rules and Tests Are Keeping Would-Be Teachers of Color out of America's Classrooms. Here's How," *Chalkbeat*, September 12, 2017, https://www.chalkbeat.org/posts/us/2017/09/12/certification-rules-and-tests-are-keeping-would-be-teachers-of-color-out-of-americas-classrooms-heres-how/.

27. Minutes of the Regular Meeting of the Massachusetts Board of Elementary and Secondary Education, May 19, 2009, https://studylib.net/doc/15155376/0519reg.

28. I attended this meeting in my capacity as a state board member.

SEVEN

Testing Concerns

This chapter explains why both teachers and parents are concerned about the use of national tests aligned to Common Core's standards. In particular, it suggests why short and frequent teacher-made tests might better help teachers to address low achievers in this country than the many tests of endurance for low achievers approved by federal policy makers and education researchers.

This chapter also suggests the use of internationally agreed-upon test items on topics in the national *curriculum* of high-achieving countries (as on Trends in International Mathematics and Science Study or TIMSS tests). Such tests will help us to compare student achievement in mathematics, science, and reading in the context that matters most for a global economy and will give low-achieving students, their teachers, and parents the best information they will ever get.

TEACHER CONCERNS

As much as Common Core's K–12 standards have been of concern to many parents, the tests based on those standards have been of possibly even greater concern—to teachers and to parents. Tests designed to assess Common Core's racist standards (no matter what the standards are officially called), as well as other sets of standards, are of utmost concern to teachers who are to be held accountable for the test scores of low achievers or "underserved learners" by means of a Value-Added Measure (VAM). A VAM is a measure of how much "value" (growth) the teacher brought to her students.

Even though ESSA tried to loosen the knot between students' scores and teacher evaluations (a knot tied by the Race to the Top application itself), there were already agreements at the local or state level (in states with or without Common Core–compliant standards) on the percentage of a teacher's evaluation that state test scores would legally be allowed to contribute or how it would contribute. A Texas judge ruled in mid-2017 that its teacher evaluation system has major flaws and poses constitutional concerns.[1] Teachers thus have reason to be concerned about being held accountable for student scores on state tests that they didn't develop or review.

The biggest problem with the tests designed to assess Common Core's standards is what the scores mean. The test items used in state tests before Common Core would in theory if not in practice have been vetted by the state's teachers (and/or by personnel at its department of education), as they were in Massachusetts. A range of teachers would have been convened at each grade level to assure other teachers, parents, and others that the test items reflected the approved standards at the grade level of the test and that, overall, the test was appropriately challenging for that grade level.

Teachers above, on, and below the grade level of the test would also have been part of the group setting the pass/fail (cut) score and determining performance level cut-offs (e.g., Advanced, Proficient, Basic). This is far more important than most people realize; pass/fail scores on K–12 student tests need to be set by some of the teachers who will be teaching students who pass the test.

Relevant teachers as standards-setters have an incentive to set the pass score at the level that makes sense for students moving to a higher grade (maybe their grade, as a Massachusetts grade ten English teacher commented at a meeting to review test items). What do *they* (teachers of a higher grade) want new students to know or be able to do?

Today, only a few people in testing companies or state education departments know for sure what is on a Common Core–compliant test, on what basis the pass/fail score was set, and who set it. In the early days of state testing in Massachusetts (before the adoption of Common Core's standards), experienced, well-read high school English teachers selected the passages for grades eight and ten and made sure the questions, answers, and distractors on multiple-choice test items were suitable and suitably challenging for each grade level. Because seasoned educators also helped to set the pass scores for all grade-level tests, parents and others could feel confident that a child who passed a grade-level test was ready for the next grade.

The problem in trying to determine what a score on a state test means when some or all of its test items are based on Common Core–compliant standards and is aggravated by the non-use, alteration, or removal of independent benchmarks (local, national, or international) to determine the validity of the scores. Both ACT and SAT have been aligned down to the level of Common Core's standards.[2] The most informative tests of all (to students and parents) have been teacher-made tests.[3] Teachers assess what they know they've taught and usually in a shorter time than state tests consume.

The down side of teacher-made tests is that teachers of the same subject may differ across classes or school districts in exactly what they teach, in their tests, and in their grading. However, despite these differences, teacher-made tests have historically been useful to high school teachers especially, because teachers know what they've taught and tend to know their students better than the scores on externally developed and computer-graded state tests suggest.

The best-known national examples of standardized tests today are the NAEP tests. (Norm-referenced tests like the Iowa Test of Basic Skills were frequently given to find out where students stood in relation to their national peers but rarely had high stakes.) There are two kinds of NAEP tests: main tests and long-term tests. Both types are considered "criterion-referenced" tests, meaning that test-takers have to get a specific number of test items right (or earn a specific number of points) to be in a specific performance category.

The main tests, begun in the early 1990s, are based on assessment standards that are occasionally revised to reflect changes in school curricula. The long-term tests began in the early 1970s and have not changed because they were designed to show trends. But the National Assessment Governing Board (NAGB) recently decided for budgetary reasons, it claimed, to defer giving the next long-term tests until 2024. The Brookings Institution published an article on this matter.[4] So has the American Enterprise Institute, essentially in agreement that NAGB's decision made no sense.[5]

Parents and Congress now have no national trend test to tell policy makers what success Common Core's standards and accountability measures have had in reducing low achievement since 2010 and what their influence on the school curriculum has been. A recognized trend line would be particularly useful at a time when changes are being urged upon the entire curriculum in the name of "personalized instruction."

Some critics of "personalized instruction" are concerned because there seems to be no strong research base supporting "adaptive practice" as a strategy for personalized instruction,[6] and costs have become controversial.[7] A Brookings Institution report credits some of the changes being made to the curriculum with the adoption of Common Core's standards.[8]

There are other reasons for retaining NAEP's long-term trends tests *and* finding old teacher-made tests to use as benchmarks (or baselines) in high school today. High school students are being urged to undertake Dual Enrollment or Early College programs *in order to accumulate college credit* before they graduate from high school, to take "co-requisites" (remedial classes accompanying regular college classes) for credit after enrollment into a college), and to decline non-credit-bearing developmental courses.

One might think that a "main" NAEP math test that has not been changed since 2009 would be useful to maintain as is, in order to show the benefits of new standards and curricula in math for low achievers. That is not the case. Even though NAEP tests are *not* supposed to be linked to specific sets of standards or pedagogy, already voices in 2017 are suggesting that the math tests should be changed to reflect the balance of topics now being taught. The suggestion has been offered as a way to address declining national average scores in grades four and eight.[9]

In addition to NAEP tests that by law only sample representative students across the country every two years or so, Trends in International Mathematics and Science Study (TIMSS), given in grades four, eight, and in high school as an advanced test, is an international test that can help this country understand the meaning of low achievement internationally, especially in science, technology, engineering, and mathematics (STEM).

TIMSS is the only international test aligned to the K–12 mathematics and science curriculum, with results that are useful for comparing STEM education in an international context. TIMSS's sponsor, the International Association for the Evaluation of Educational Achievement (IEA), also conducts the Progress in International Reading Literacy Study (PIRLS), an international study of reading achievement in fourth graders.

However, the U.S. Department of Education (USED) seems to be more interested in the Programme for International Student Assessment (PISA), a test of skills in fifteen-year olds, with mathematical content judged at about the grade five/six level. (The director of PISA assessments—Andreas Schleicher—was a member of Common Core's Validation Committee.) For exactly how TIMSS and PISA differ in the information each provides to parents and teachers (depending on the particular countries that participate in a particular year), see the 2009 monograph by the Thomas B. Fordham Institute describing all these tests.[10]

PARENT CONCERNS

Parents have also expressed concerns about other aspects of currently mandated federal/state tests—that they assess subjectively judged skills through competency-based testing and raise privacy concerns.[11] Parents are concerned as well about the mandate for "computer-adaptive" testing (something that is not easy for the average parent or teacher to understand when trying to compare student achievement scores).[12]

In general, parents' concerns have been ignored by USED, many governors, and state legislatures. Their indifference was particularly egregious in Massachusetts, the state that had the most to lose when its state board of education adopted gap-closing standards in 2010 in place of standards that had increased the academic achievement of all groups in the state. Its pre–Common Core standards had been designed to help teachers to raise all students' academic achievement (which they did), not to close gaps. But Massachusetts voted in gap-closing standards because it had been promised $250,000,000 in Race to the Top (RttT) funds.

The game played by the state board and the secretary of education in the context of the Massachusetts Education Reform Act or MERA, 1993, a law requiring state tests based on state standards, began in November 2015. That was when the Massachusetts Board of Education agreed to a "compromise" on what to call a Common Core–aligned state test. It could choose between a test called PARCC (Partnership for the Assessment of Readiness for College and Career, and a test called MCAS (Massachusetts Comprehensive Assessment System) mandated in MERA and until 2010 based on the state's pre–Common Core standards.

By 2015, MCAS was based solely on Common Core's standards, which the Board of Elementary and Secondary Education had adopted in 2010. The board's "compromise" was to call the one test it would henceforth administer MCAS 2.0—or "next generation MCAS." However, the board's decision ended up confusing more than Massachusetts residents or the media, as will be clear shortly.

The compromise (over what to call a Common Core–aligned state test in a state that mandated a state test) grew out of a long-simmering controversy over the use of Common Core's standards and the PARCC tests. The controversy had led a statewide group of mainly parents to collect signatures to try to place a question on the November 2016 ballot allowing voters to decide whether they wanted to keep Common Core's standards and tests.

Gates Foundation grants to the Massachusetts Business Alliance for Education (over $400,000, according to an article in Bay State Parent[13]) had enabled the MBAE, a small organization that had played *no* role in the development of the state's first-class pre-Common Core standards, to hire Foley Hoag, a very expensive law firm in Boston. The purpose was to challenge the constitutionality of the possible ballot question.

Ironically, the Massachusetts Attorney General's office had declared the question constitutional in 2014 and appropriate for the ballot. Nevertheless, Justice Margot Botsford on the state's Supreme Judicial Court agreed with Foley Hoag's peculiar legal reasoning that the release of used test items (one of four sections in the ballot question) was unrelated to a test's transparency and took away the opportunity for the state's voters to decide on the use of Common Core's standards and tests in their own public schools.

In sum, Justice Botsford declared unconstitutional the question that the Attorney General's office had declared constitutional a year earlier. In addition, she apparently persuaded colleagues on the court to follow her (and Foley Hoag's) reasoning.

MCAS 2.0 tests were given to Bay State students in March and April 2017. At this time, Rhode Island's Department of Education decided to adopt these tests in place of PARCC's tests, which had also been used in Rhode Island. There, too, they were disliked by parents. Even though MCAS 2.0 consists mainly of PARCC test items and has been called PARCC in disguise, we do not know even today if Rhode Island state officials really believe that tests called MCAS 2.0 resemble the original MCAS tests in any way.

Insiders know that they bear no resemblance. For example, the original MCAS tests featured four teacher-corrected "Open Response" items at every tested grade level. But Rhode Island's commissioner of education and his staff have so far told parents little about the source or format of the test items in MCAS 2.0. And reporters may not be able to tell them the truth—just that the "new" test looks a lot like the old PARCC test.[14]

What is likely is that PARCC's sale of its test items to Rhode Island (and possibly to other states in the future), on the deceptive grounds that tests called MCAS today are different from tests known to be aligned to Common Core's standards, would get PARCC out of its current financial hole. More important, it could serve the goal of nationalizing public education in this country.

Other states might be encouraged to commit to tests called MCAS in the future, with common test items developed by PARCC and pass/fail scores determined by wizards behind a green curtain at USED. All this might make parents everywhere think their state was using the original MCAS tests and the standards on which they had been based. A "*grande illusion*," to be sure.

In the meantime, there has been *no* transparency about who, if anyone, has vetted the contents of Common Core–aligned tests against the content of TIMSS tests in science and mathematics (tests independent of USED and Common Core–oriented foundations in this country). Nor is there any transparency about who specifically determines the pass scores for all performance levels of "college readiness" tests in high school and for the SAT, ACT, and ACT-Aspire tests that have now been aligned (down) to Common Core's high school standards.

Yet, locally elected school boards may allow the teachers they hire to be evaluated in part on student scores on these tests. And college admission officers may use these scores as evidence of college readiness, or be required to.

KEY IDEAS TO REMEMBER

1. Educators have many concerns about the use of tests aligned to Common Core's standards (e.g., PARCC, SBAC, SAT, ACT Aspire) for evaluating teachers and rating students.

2. From parents' perspectives, Common Core-compliant tests are mainly skills- or competency-based and, as such, have no clear and accepted academic meaning. Parents also worry about the instructional time spent on teaching to national- or state-mandated tests or test items.

NOTES

1. Derek Black, "Federal Court Finds Texas Teacher Evaluation System Is a 'House of Cards,' Issuing Ruling That Helps It Fall," LPB Network, August 9, 2017, http://lawprofessors.typepad.com/education_law/2017/08/federal-court-finds-texas-teacher-evaluation-system-is-a-house-of-cards-issuing-ruling-that-helps-it.html.

2. Paul Mittermeier, "Is the SAT Aligning to Common Core Standards?," *The Collegian*, April 7, 2016, http://hillsdalecollegian.com/2016/04/is-the-sat-aligning-to-common-core-standards/.

3. As one example, see "The Advantages of Teacher-Made Tests," *Seattle PI*, 2017, http://education.seattlepi.com/advantages-teachermade-tests-1595.html.

4. Tom Loveless, "The Strange Case of the Disappearing NAEP," Brookings Institution, Monday, October 17, 2016, https://www.brookings.edu/blog/brown-center-chalkboard/2016/10/17/the-strange-case-of-the-disappearing-naep/.

5. Nat Malkus, "The Disappearing Excuse for the Disappearing NAEP," AEIdeas, October 24, 2016, https://www.aei.org/publication/the-disappearing-excuse-for-the-disappearing-naep/.

6. Dan Willingham, "Adaptive Practice and Personalized Learning and What Will 'Obviously' Work in Education," *Science & Education* (blog), June 5, 2017, http://www.danielwillingham.com/daniel-willingham-science-and-education-blog/adaptive-practice-personalized-learning-and-what-will-obviously-work-in-education.

7. Sri Ravipati, "Report: Schools Are Being Duped by Marketers on Personalized Learning," *The Journal*, August 22, 2017, https://thejournal.com/articles/2017/08/22/report-schools-are-being-duped-by-marketers-on-personalized-learning.aspx?m=1.

8. Tom Loveless, "2016 Brown Center Report on American Education: How Well Are American Students Learning?" Brookings Institution, Thursday, March 24, 2016, https://www.brookings.edu/research/2016-brown-center-report-on-american-education-how-well-are-american-students-learning/.

9. David Bressoud, "The 2015 NAEP," *Launchings* (blog), July 5, 2017, http://launchings.blogspot.com/2017/07/the-2015-naep.html.

10. Sheila Byrd Carmichael, W. Stephen Wilson, Chester E. Finn Jr., Amber M. Winkler, and Stafford Palmieri, *Stars by Which to Navigate? An Interim Report on Common Core, NAEP, TIMSS, and PISA* (Washington, DC: Thomas B. Fordham Institute, October 2009), http://www.math.jhu.edu/~wsw/papers/20091008_NationalStandards.pdf.

11. Karen Effrem, "Specific Concerns about Competency Based Ed. in SB 1714 Related to Cost, Quality, Privacy and Choice," *Florida Stop Common Core Coalition*, March 4, 2016, http://www.flstopcccoalition.org/blog/specific-concerns-about-competency-based-ed-sb-1714-related-cost-quality-privacy-choice.htm.

12. Lawrence M. Rudner, "An On-line, Interactive, Computer Adaptive Testing Tutorial ," November 1998, http://echo.edres.org:8080/scripts/cat/catdemo.htm.

13. Doug Page, "The Surprising Backers Behind Common Core in Massachusetts," *BayStateParent Magazine*, September 1, 2015, https://www.baystateparent.com/2015/09/01/the-surprising-backers-behind-common-core-in-massachusetts/.

14. Dan McGowan, "RI's New Standardized Test Is Similar to PARCC, but Shorter," Eyewitness News, WPRI.com, September 4, 2017, http://wpri.com/2017/09/04/ris-new-standardized-test-is-similar-to-parcc-but-shorter/.

EIGHT
What Might Desperate Education Policy Makers Do?

So far, none of the changes now being "implemented" in K–12 public education, especially since 1965, has done much to increase the achievement of large numbers of low-achieving groups of students. In fact, some of the changes made in the name of reform, such as more testing, may have decelerated their intellectual growth or retarded the possibility of much of an increase.

What Congress or state legislatures should beware of are desperate attempts by self-appointed education policy makers to establish policies that, they claim, will show the policies they have enacted to have worked, not failed, or to continue insisting that more funds be made available for them. This chapter suggests what some of the new policies may be and why they won't work.

WHY NEW IDEAS ARE NEEDED

Expressing increases in achievement as declines in a "test-score gap"—perhaps to remind readers that the "test-score gap" between groups in academic achievement is what matters to researchers, not academic achievement itself—economist Eric Hanushek in a 2016 article noted,

> In both math and reading, the national test-score gap in 1965 was 1.1 standard deviations, implying that the average black 12th grader placed at the 13th percentile of the score distribution for white students. In other words, 87 percent of white 12th graders scored ahead of the average black 12th grader. What does it look like 50 years later? In math, the size of the gap has fallen nationally by 0.2 standard deviations, but that still leaves the average black 12th-grade student at only

the 19th percentile of the white distribution. In reading, the achievement gap has improved slightly more than in math (0.3 standard deviations), but after a half century, the average black student scores at just the 22nd percentile of the white distribution.[1]

Despite researchers' obsession with white achievement, today we need to pay as much attention to the "national test-score gap" between "Asian Americans" and blacks as to the test-score gap between whites and blacks. (They need, above all, to pay attention to the average American student's low level of achievement regardless of race or ethnicity.)

In his 2016 article on student achievement, written for a commemorative issue of *Education Next* on James Coleman's 1966 report *Equality of Educational Opportunity* (a report mandated by the Civil Rights Act of 1964 and issued about fifty years ago), Hanushek noted two of the well-known findings of the Coleman Report:

1. "Variations in per-pupil expenditure had little correlation with student outcomes."
2. Teacher quality mattered. But "whether teachers are certified, or obtain an advanced degree, or attend a specific college or university, or receive more or less mentoring or professional development turns out to be almost completely unrelated to a teacher's effectiveness in the classroom."

Generally speaking, little attention has been paid by policy makers to the first finding. Unfortunately, echoes of what "excellence in instruction" meant in the Houston, Texas, 2011 Apollo program can be heard in the comment on teacher quality (a concept that is being promoted to mean teacher effectiveness in a classroom).

The central conclusion to be drawn from Coleman's 1966 report in Hanushek's eyes is this:

> That schools bring little influence to bear on a child's achievement that is independent of his background and general social context; and that this very lack of an independent effect means that the inequalities imposed on children by their home, neighborhood, and peer environment are carried along to become the inequalities with which they confront adult life at the end of school.

If no educational program/strategy seems to work, or work quickly, in addressing massive low achievement in a nationally important demographic group, then why aren't researchers trying to develop policies to address the "inequalities" imposed by children's home, neighborhood, and peer environment? What are these inequalities, to begin with? In other words, why aren't researchers in education or in other areas helping policy makers to explore what the Coleman Report indicated was a major source of low achievement in black students? Perhaps massive low achievement in K–12 for a larger number of demographic groups has not had and will not have educational solutions because its causes aren't chiefly the schools that low-achieving children now attend or the minor differences between the resources now allocated to their schools and others', or between the teachers they and others now have.

Interestingly, one and only one of the "inequalities" imposed by families, neighborhoods, and peers seems to have been addressed, however unevenly, through social policies. Integration of differently populated school districts is one way to address a Coleman Report finding that the peer environment in a low-performing school was a cause of low student achievement. But although there are some studies showing the positive effects of socioeconomic integration of different school populations on student achievement,[2] it did not have the same effects everywhere.[3]

Desegregation in Boston and elsewhere in the form of redrawn school attendance boundary lines and compulsory busing did not lead (immediately or ultimately) to higher achievement for the chiefly low-achieving students left behind after middle-class white and black parents placed their children in private schools or moved elsewhere.[4] In Boston it led to a higher concentration of low-achieving children in most of its public schools. As an August 2016 Brookings Institution article concluded, it is not at all clear that the social and educational benefits of "integration" outweighed or would outweigh the costs.[5]

The lack of interest or courage in exploring the formulation of public policies to address the "inequalities" imposed on children by their home environment has had serious consequences for the public schools. It is extremely difficult to find concrete recommendations for addressing the inequality that children face who grow up in single-parent, not two-parent, families—the situation, it seems, in most African American homes since the 1990s.[6]

Almost all studies of children's achievement as it relates to growing up in two-parent versus single-parent families show strong differences on average favoring the former.[7] Recommendations can be found, but they don't seem to be aimed at reducing that kind of inequality. Documenting the strengths of single parents, or helping single parents and their children make the best of their situation, or increasing their income deserves commendation, but none seeks to reduce the formation of young single-parent families.[8]

Nor can recommendations be found that address a long-standing finding of the research on low achievement.[9] The U.S. National Institutes of Health found "that a mother's reading skill is the greatest determinant of her children's future academic success, outweighing other factors, such as neighborhood and family income." Policies to improve all mothers' reading skills don't address single-parenting but they might address their children's low achievement better than current education policies do.

It is not that policy makers should not try to improve the image of current single parents or to build up their self-esteem for their and their children's sake. The problem is that none of the recommendations to be found focuses on ways to reduce the likelihood of single-parenting, particularly important because boys seem to be more damaged than girls by the absence of a stable father in their homes while growing up.

WHY SOME OF THE LATEST IDEAS ARE UNLIKELY TO WORK

Because none of the changes in educational structures for K–16 or in K–16 curriculum or pedagogy made over the twentieth century quickly increased (if at all) the achievement of large numbers of low achievers, other possibilities for a "quick fix" have occasionally emerged as suggestions or as implications of current education policies as some see them. Although these education ideas, too, are unlikely to work, education policy makers will likely try to promote something to salvage their self-esteem. Congress should beware of schemes that propose the following:

1. Hold the faculty in teacher preparation programs accountable for the performance of their graduates who teach in K–12 schools, based on their students' scores on federally mandated K–12 tests. Beware because: licensure tests were designed for that purpose, and they are the tests that need to be strengthened.
2. Align all tests used in this country to Common Core's standards. Beware because: these standards were designed to close "gaps," not to strengthen public education.
3. Avoid using independent, curriculum-aligned tests (e.g., TIMSS for grades four, eight and Advanced TIMSS; PIRLS) with the claim that they are too costly. Beware because: independent, curriculum-based tests that randomly sample all students *are* the best if not only way this country can find out how much damage gap-closing standards have done to the public schools.
4. Use skills-based tests only (e.g., PISA) with the claim that this is what twenty-first-century employers want. Beware because: these kinds of tests tell teachers almost nothing about what is missing in the curriculum.
5. Change achievement norms to reduce test-score gaps with the claim that higher-achieving groups "overperform" or "overachieve." Beware because: norms need to come from students in high-achieving countries that American students will compete against—on independent, curriculum-aligned tests like TIMSS.
6. Prepare all students in public schools for the workforce with the claim that well-paying jobs are what most parents want. Beware because: most parents anywhere do not favor workforce prepara-

tion for all students in place of optional high school curricula or student-selected postsecondary goals.

Few if any parents in the United States have lauded Common Core's effects on their children's learning or the K–8 curriculum. Indeed, few observers see anything worthwhile in the standards funded by the Melinda and Bill Gates Foundation and promoted by the organizations it has subsidized to promote them (e.g., the Thomas B. Fordham Institute, the U.S. Chamber of Commerce, and Jeb Bush's Foundation for Educational Excellence). Criticism of the effects of its English language arts standards on the school curriculum and public life is often by parents who have decided to homeschool.[10]

Joy Pullmann's *The Education Invasion: How Common Core Fights Parents for Control of American Kids* is a recent addition to the critics' side of the Common Core controversy.[11] Her purpose is to explain what Common Core is and how it got to be implemented in almost every state in a remarkably short period of time (less than five years). She does so chiefly from the perspective of the many parents and teachers she quotes.

Organized in seven chapters, her book describes how the Melinda and Bill Gates Foundation promoted one extremely wealthy couple's uninformed, unsupported, and unsupportable ideas on education for other people's children while their own children are enrolled in a non-Common Core private school. It explains why parents, teachers, local school boards, and state legislators were the last to learn how the policies affecting the schools supported by their taxes had been shaped by a federal agency without congressional permission.

It also explains why parents and others were expected to believe that their local public schools were now accountable for what and how they teach, not to the local and state taxpayers who fund them or to locally elected school boards who are legally charged with setting their policies, but to a distant bureaucracy. Their local public schools were now to be accountable to this distant bureaucracy for the use of some of their own tax money in closing "achievement gaps" between unspecified groups based on standards and tests teachers and parents didn't want in the first place.

Overnight, teachers discovered they were accountable to anonymous bureaucrats for students' scores on tests these teachers had not developed or reviewed, before or after their administration. Amazingly, state boards and governors believed the state's teachers were accountable to the U.S. Department of Education despite the fact that the federal government pays for only about 8 to 10 percent of the costs of public education on average across states, and not for teachers' or superintendents' salaries.

Pullmann's book carefully tells the complex story of how English language arts and mathematics standards (and, later, compatible science standards) were created by non-standards experts selected chiefly (so far as we know) by the Gates Foundation. She doesn't tell us why these standards were so quickly adopted by mathematically ignorant state boards of education.

But what is chiefly missing is an analysis of how the peer-review process for approving a state plan under the Every Student Succeeds Act (ESSA) ensures continuing federal control of a state's public schools via gap-closing or racist standards. A subsequent blog post explains how Common Core's standards have ironically come to limit if not damage the education of all children, including those it claims to want to make "college ready."[12]

Senator Lamar Alexander of Tennessee, ESSA's major sponsor in Congress, often declared his intention to reduce federal control of public education and restore a modicum of control to local government. But ESSA gives parents or state/local taxpayers little opportunity to shape the guidelines for their own public school curriculum or report cards. Instead, it mandates that all state departments of education submit a four-year State Plan that must be approved by the U.S. Department of Education in 2017 in order to get federal funds.

A State Plan developed by a state's unelected department of education indicates what the state will commit to for at least four years, regardless of cost, to address ESSA's many requirements for closing "achievement gaps," including the standards and tests it will use for all students in its public schools. Strangely, there was no public debate or media analysis of how the left hand took away what the right hand (Sen. Alexander's intention) gave.

The deceptive strategies used by Rhode Island and Massachusetts in 2015–2017 to pretend they are mandating better tests than those overtly aligned to Common Core's standards (implying the K–12 curriculum would be strengthened) suggest the game that may be embedded in ESSA's approved State Plans for these states. See chapter 7 on testing concerns for details.

Current concerns in education seem to be based on the little if any narrowing of the gap since 1965,[13] not on educational outcomes for most students. After ACT reported in 2017 that only 9 percent of "underserved learners" were strongly college ready,[14] a September 6, 2017, article in the *Washington Post* on ACT's report quoted a spokesman for Education Trust, a pro–Common Core organization, that "[s]tates and schools . . . must redouble efforts to narrow and eliminate achievement gaps." Why the billions spent since 1965, including use of college and career-readiness standards and tests, hadn't made a difference was not discussed.

The ACT report was more fully discussed by Shane Vander Hart on the blogsite *Truth in Education*.[15] But no one asked why so many students who were so unready for college (almost half) were taking the ACT to begin with.

To sum up, there is no evidence that the federal government has done better than local governments in improving the education and well-being of low-achieving children. There is no evidence that giving more money to the parents or schools of low-achieving students or increasing "accessibility" improved their academic record or social status as adolescents despite a few changes up and down, or plateaus, in early grades. So why a continued belief in the value of centralized policy making in education?

There is nothing historical or empirical to support the feasibility of ESEA's changed goals in the Every Student Succeeds Act (to close achievement gaps, not to strengthen the public education system). Yet Congress required staff at a state department of education to submit a four-year plan to the U.S. Department of Education to address federal goals of "closed gaps." Nor is there any constitutional basis for a state education department staff or state board of education committing hundreds of locally elected school boards to these federal goals (in exchange for federal funds) without their permission or the approval of their own state legislature.

"Closed gaps," whatever it means, is not an educational goal and, if at all obtainable, cannot be achieved by education policies. What does it take to get educators and policy makers to understand that?

NOTES

1. Eric Hanushek, "What Matters for Student Achievement—Updating Coleman on the Influence of Families and Schools," *Education Next* 16, no. 2 (Spring 2016), http://educationnext.org/what-matters-for-student-achievement/.

2. Amy Stuart Wells, Lauren Fox, and Diana Cordova-Cobo, "The Benefits of Socioeconomically and Racially Integrated Schools and Classrooms," The Century Foundation, February 10, 2016, https://tcf.org/content/facts/the-benefits-of-socioeconomically-and-racially-integrated-schools-and-classrooms/; http://www.journals.uchicago.edu/doi/abs/10.1086/227761.

3. Willis Hawley, "Critical Thinking Skills and Academic Achievement," *Teaching Tolerance*, n.d., https://www.tolerance.org/professional-development/critical-thinking-skills-and-academic-achievement; Susan Eaton and Steven Rivkin, " Is Desegregation Dead? Parsing the Relationship between Achievement and Demographics," *Education Next* 10, no. 4 (Fall 2010), http://educationnext.org/is-desegregation-dead/; and Michael Hansen, "In Search of the Key to Closing Achievement Gaps," *U.S.News*, January 8, 2016, https://www.usnews.com/opinion/knowledge-bank/articles/2016-01-08/the-academic-benefit-of-reducing-school-segregation-may-be-overblown/.

4. Paul Delaney, "Black Middle Class Joining the Exodus To White Suburbia," *New York Times*, January 4, 1976,http://www.nytimes.com/1976/01/04/archives/black-middle-class-joining-the-exodus-to-white-suburbia-black.html.

5. David Armor, "Bringing Back Busing: Do Benefits Outweigh Cost?," Brookings Institution, August 23, 2016, https://www.brookings.edu/blog/brown-center-chalkboard/2016/08/23/bringing-back-busing-do-benefits-outweigh-cost/.

6. James T. Patterson , "Moynihan and the Single-Parent Family—the 1965 Report and Its Backlash," *Education Next* 15, no. 2 (Spring 2015), http://educationnext.org/moynihan-and-the-single-parent-family/.

7. For example, "Children in Single-Parent Families Perform Worse on Achievement Tests than Their Two-Parent Peers," National Center for Policy Analysis, January 28, 2015, http://www.ncpa.org/sub/dpd/index.php?Article_ID=25300; and Sara McClanahan, "The Consequences of Single Motherhood," *American Prospect*, Summer 1994, http://prospect.org/article/consequences-single-motherhood.

8. Mark Barajas, "Academic Achievement of Children in Single Parent Homes: A Critical Review," *Hilltop Review* 5, no, 1 (2011): 12–21, http://scholarworks.wmich.edu/cgi/viewcontent.cgi?article=1044&context=hilltopreview.

9. U.S. Department of Heath and Human Services, "Improving Mothers' Literacy Skills May Be the Best Way to Boost Children's Achievement," October 25, 2010, http://www.nih.gov/news/health/oct2010/nichd-25.htm.

10. Lisa Hudson, "Why Common Core's Lack of Literature Is Setting Kids Up for Failure," *The National Pulse*, August 22, 2017, https://thenationalpulse.com/commentary/why-common-core-lack-fiction-reading-setting-kids-failure/.

11. Joy Pullman, *The Education Invasion: How Common Core Fights Parents for Control of American Kids* (New York: Encounter Books, 2017).

12. Joy Pullmann, "How Common Core Damages Students' College Readiness," James G. Martin Center, March 10, 2017, https://www.jamesgmartin.center/2017/03/common-core-damages-students-college-readiness/.

13. Lauren Camera, "Achievement Gap between White and Black Students Still Gaping. After 50 Years, the Achievement Gap between White and Black Students Has Barely Narrowed," *USNews*, January 13, 2016, https://www.usnews.com/news/blogs/data-mine/2016/01/13/achievement-gap-between-white-and-black-students-still-gaping.

14. "The Condition of College and Career Readiness 2017," ACT, http://www.act.org/content/act/en/research/condition-of-college-and-career-readiness-2017.html.

15. Shane Vander Hart, "ACT CEO: Current Education System Is Not Working Well Enough," *Truth in American Education*, September 8, 2017,https://truthinamericaneducation.com/education-reform/act-ceo-current-education-system-is-not-working/?utm_campaign=shareaholic&utm_medium=twitter&utm_source=socialnetwork.

NINE

What Can State Legislatures with a Spine Do?

Possibilities

This chapter sums up what several experts on education see as central issues to address in order to strengthen public education in this country, keep students from dropping out of high school, and reduce low achievement. It suggests what state legislatures can do and then points out a few large-scale reform programs that have empirically raised the academic achievement of students who participated in them. It concludes with suggestions for possible solutions to vast adolescent underachievement.

HIGH COSTS AND LITTLE RETURN ON THE INVESTMENT

Few education researchers and educators can dispute the high costs of public education today—and its mediocre quality. In Andrew Coulson's words, written in 2011, "To sum up, we have little to show for the $2 trillion in federal education spending of the past half century. In the face of concerted and unflagging efforts by Congress and the states, public schooling has suffered a massive productivity collapse—it now costs three times as much to provide essentially the same education as we provided in 1970."[1] In another essay, published in March 2014, he further commented that

> there has been essentially no correlation between what states have spent on education and their measured academic outcomes. In other words, America's educational productivity appears to have collapsed, at least as measured by the NAEP and the SAT. . . . Two generations seems a long time for a field to stand outside of history, particularly

when those generations have witnessed so many reforms aimed at improving education. Perhaps it's time to ask if there are inherent features in our approach to schooling that prevent it from enjoying the progress typical in other fields.[2]

In a partial answer to Coulson's query, we need to go back a half a century. In a retrospective essay published in 2000 on the Sputnik-Era Curriculum Reform movement of the 1950s and 1960s, Mary Campbell Gallagher pointed to two features of our system of public education that have resisted serious efforts at academic reform in the past fifty years—the school curriculum and teacher training:

> If good curricula are to drive out bad, as we all hope, our experience in the Curriculum Reform movement shows that the contributions of scholars and scientists are necessary to make good curricula. However, scholars' intellectual authority alone does not suffice for the long term. We need excellent teacher training more than we need anything else. We need to train teachers in subject matter, and to teach them how to teach our lessons while they are still in training. We need to give in-service teachers both solid training in subject matter and the kinds of lessons they want to teach. We need to show them how to teach these lessons, and to give them day-to-day support.[3]

What are essential problems with the school curriculum? (Chapter 6 addresses issues in teacher quality.) There is widespread agreement about the lack of adequate content in the K–12 curriculum at all grade levels. E. D. Hirsch's 2016 book, *Why Knowledge Matters: Rescuing Our Children from Failed Educational Theories*, draws on findings in neuroscience and data from France to argue for reforming elementary curricula.[4]

However, despite the fact that Hirsch's book received consistently positive reviews, it's hard to find one school district in this country developing any part of its K–12 curriculum, or a state department of education that has developed a four-year state plan with reference to Hirsch or his ideas.[5]

In state plans submitted for the Every Student Succeeds Act (ESSA), it's just as difficult to find a reference to the pre–Common Core Massachusetts standards in English language arts or mathematics, which played a major role in boosting that state's students into first place in 2005 on National Assessment of Educational Progress (NAEP) reading *and* mathematics tests for grades four and eight. Students in Massachusetts have stayed in first place or near the top at both grade levels since 2005.

The state's pre–Common Core standards in both subjects also undergirded students' very high scores on the Trends in International Mathematics and Science Study (TIMSS) mathematics tests for grades four and eight in 2007 and 2011 (including a first-place tie in both years with

Singapore in grade eight science) when the state participated in TIMSS as a separate country.

Interestingly, the Massachusetts commissioner and/or secretary of education chose to discontinue the state's participation in TIMSS in 2015—even though TIMSS is the only test aligned to internationally agreed-upon topics for study in the K–12 mathematics and science curriculum—in favor of participation in a test based on reading and math skills for fifteen-year olds (Program for International Student Assessment, or PISA) that uses below-grade-level content and provides no useful information to teachers or parents.

It seems that tests providing useful information to teachers and students (in math and in science) (i.e., curriculum-oriented information) in an international context have not been desired by federal or state education policy makers despite our participation as a country in a "global economy."

U.S. Department of Education (USED) peer reviewers have also shown no interest in empirically effective K–12 standards. None of the reviewers of the first drafts of state plans sent to USED since April 2017, so far as has been reported, has called for academically stronger state standards in the final plan.[6] For example, for its review of submitted ESSA plans in April 2017, "Mapping Career Readiness in State ESSA Plans—Round 1," the Thomas B. Fordham Institute did not develop or use one criterion on the quality of proposed state standards, or report any comments to the effect that they need to be strengthened in any state.[7] (Nor did Fordham reviewers explain why its title mysteriously describes the plans as addressing "careers" only, not "college and career readiness.") Most submitted state standards are aligned to Common Core's standards in English, mathematics, and science, no matter what their name is, and they are for both "college" and "career" and inadequate for both.[8]

Evidence for the inadequacies comes first and foremost from the staying power of Massachusetts students' rise to first place in 2005 in two different subjects and at two different grade levels on NAEP tests (and the current and detectable beginnings of decline). Although the Massachusetts Board of Elementary and Secondary Education voted for Common Core's ELA and math standards in 2010 (for the promise of $250,000,000 in RttT grants), and these standards were implemented in 2013, the state was clearly reaping the benefits of both first-rate K–12 standards/tests, all of which were developed long before 2010, and academically stronger K–12 teachers. The state got academically stronger teachers from its revised teacher licensure regulations in 2000, revised subject matter licensure tests in the early 2000s especially for prospective Early Childhood and Elementary teachers, and content-focused criteria for professional development.

In addition, while it is not difficult to find teachers or administrators quoted for their laudatory remarks on Common Core's English language arts standards (or attesting to their virtues in public testimony), it is impossible to find any positive reference to Common Core's English language arts standards by recognized literary scholars or composition experts. Former New Hampshire State Board of Education member Bill Duncan is notorious for a unique attempt to discredit me, Sandra Stotsky, as the leading critic of Common Core's English language arts standards (in a recently disabled link),[9] as well as James Milgram, the leading critic of its mathematics standards,[10] misleading uninformed readers of his blog who might assume that other national experts find something praiseworthy in them.

But there is little or no praise for Common Core's English language arts standards or the tests based on them in the observations of three highly regarded tenured or retired professors of English: Mark Bauerlein, Emory University;[11] E. D. Hirsch, University of Virginia;[12] and Thomas Newkirk, University of New Hampshire.[13] Nor can one find even one noted literary or composition scholar with a kind word for the reading and writing standards that two non-experts (David Coleman and Sue Pimentel[14]) created and imposed on the nation's children with the help of the Bill and Melinda Gates Foundation, the USED's Race to the Top grant competition in 2010, and the Council for Chief State School Officers (CCSSO)—and who have been handsomely rewarded financially for their work (in Coleman's case, with the presidency of the College Board and a salary its board of trustees thought would prod him to make the SAT more competitive with the ACT).

The situation is similar in mathematics. Neither of the two national organizations for mathematicians in the country (or the many organizations for scientists and for engineers) has provided a review and praise for Common Core's mathematics standards. In fact, a Berkeley mathematician denounced them in the *Wall Street Journal*.[15]

WHAT STATE LEGISLATURES CAN DO, WITH OR WITHOUT FEDERAL PERMISSION

We lack recommendations for addressing large groups of low achievers in our public schools that take into account the possibility that the roots of vast low achievement in young adolescents are not susceptible to quick alteration by federal, state, or local educational policies, whether or not accompanied by programs that address the home environment. For example, in his testimony to a congressional committee in 2011 explaining why we have gotten almost nothing in return for the trillions this country has invested in public education in the past fifty years, Andrew Coulson recommended Opportunity Scholarships for Washington, D.C., students (a district for which Congress has legal educational oversight).[16] While private scholarship programs are not subject to federal guidelines and might spur low-achieving students to make greater efforts in their academic studies than they now do, they do not change students' home environment or the federal guidelines in approved state plans and the various sections of ESSA affecting all public schools and their students.

It is useful to recall that there are education policies for strengthening local public school curricula that could be formulated by state legislatures and that do not violate ESSA or restrict parents' influence on their local public school curriculum and the pedagogy used in them via their own elected school boards. State legislatures do not need federal permission to legally address the following concerns.

The increasingly lower academic quality of our teaching corps. Parent participation in setting pass/fail scores for Early Childhood and Elementary teacher licenses can be mandated. Admission and exit standards for publicly supported teacher/administrator preparation programs are also a state responsibility, and parent participation in setting pass/fail scores on state–approved licensure tests can be mandated by state legislatures.

Prospective teachers' poor training or lack of training in teaching beginning reading and arithmetic skills, and historical/geographical/civic knowledge. State legislatures can mandate effective and nondiscriminatory curriculum materials to be used in publicly supported elementary teacher/administrator preparation programs (since they fund them) and in a state-required history course in K–12. In 1993, the Massachusetts legislature required the reading of *The Federalist Papers* in K–12 but did not specify when or how specific selections should be taught.

Misplacement of socio-emotional learning (SEL) standards in the public school curriculum.[17] State legislatures can require public schools to remove them. Such standards have no academic content and do not belong in a school's academic curriculum. Their use is problematic with or without a child psychiatrist or clinical psychologist to inspect and approve test items addressing them on school assessments or to supervise classroom teachers who are told to address them as part of the school's academic curriculum.

Implementation of standards for mental health based largely on public health or medical research require the participation of trained medical or psychological personnel for their development, administration, and interpretation, whether they are used on tests or in classrooms. The major organization promoting SEL standards and programs for K–12 schools (CASEL) offers not *one* example of a high-quality classroom-based study based on teachers' use of them in regular classrooms. Most of the "evidence-based" studies CASEL offers are not classroom-based, and CASEL's advisory board lists not one child psychiatrist or clinical psychologist.[18]

Federal ban on freshman placement tests in public colleges. Despite agreements by college administrators in Race to the Top applications prepared by their state departments of K–12 instruction in 2010 to eliminate college freshman placement tests, state legislatures can mandate their use in colleges supported by state taxpayers. These tests help faculty in publicly funded state or community colleges to plan appropriate precollege coursework for students who have been admitted but do not have the necessary knowledge or skills for credit-bearing college-level coursework.[19]

Lack of accountability plans in ESSA's required State Plan for most of the money used for K–12 public schooling in a state. About 90 percent of the costs of our public schools are borne by local and state taxpayers, and accountability plans have yet to be formulated for the funds for local school costs coming from local and state agencies. So far, only test-based accountability plans have been formulated in ESSA's State Plan, and only for the funds coming from USED—about 10 percent of the costs. State legislatures can mandate that their department of education develop other forms of accountability to USED (not just test-based accountability), and that locally elected school boards develop accountability plans for all the agencies or legislative bodies in a state that provide the bulk of the funds for the schools under their jurisdiction.

Lack of qualifications for student enrollment in publicly funded Advanced Placement courses. State legislatures can spell out the kinds of qualifications that all schools must require before allowing students to enroll in Advanced Placement courses paid for by the state (or, if the state pays the fees, for AP tests it may require students to take).

Mediocre K–12 standards approved by a state board of education. State legislatures can demand that the state's current standards be revised to show that they address or avoid the damage that current standards seem to be causing and how.[20] The highly touted pre–Common Core English language arts standards in Massachusetts had several notable features: (1) they aimed all students for high school–level reading in high school; (2) they stressed the reading of literary texts in the secondary years (but not to the exclusion of nonliterary texts); (3) they prioritized reading over writing (because writing has a dependent relationship on reading as research and experience indicate); (4) reading passages were selected and/or vetted by the state's own English teachers; (5) short paragraphs of reading-based writing at every tested grade level, as well as lengthy compositions at three different grade levels, were corrected/rated by the state's own English teachers; and (6) all used test items were made available to parents as well as teachers each year.

Lack of constitutionality of the federal guidelines in their state.[21] A state legislature can vote to require a joint committee on education (involving both the State House and the State Senate) to review all federal guidelines in education to determine whether or not they are constitutional or excessive and what to do with their findings.

Inappropriate procedures that may have been used by the state's board and department of education and governor to entice the state to adopt and implement Common Core–aligned standards and nontransparent tests based on them.[22] A state legislature can vote to require a joint committee on education (involving both the State House and the State Senate) to review the procedures used in the state by the state's board and department of K–12 education and governor to get a state to adopt and implement Common Core–aligned standards and nontransparent tests based on them (nontransparent in the sense that it is not public knowledge who developed and vetted the test items and set the pass/fail scores for the different performance levels).

Limited or lack of meaningful educational choices in local school districts. State legislatures can mandate that all local school districts must allow education choices to include the classroom curriculum in K–8 and the high school curriculum in 9–12, not just building management or vouchers or savings accounts. No state can confine its parents to education choices mandated by the federal government, especially when the federal government has no constitutional authority to formulate any guidelines on "choice" and only contributes 10 percent of the costs of public education.

Limited number of career/technical education high schools in their state. If there was one thing that education researchers could have advised the (unknown) ESSA writers on, it was the demonstrated value of curriculum choice at the high school level in Massachusetts. The state's thirty regional vocational/technical high schools have had almost a 100 percent pass rate for its students on state tests since 2000, huge waiting lists for most of them, and almost no attrition from grade nine to grade twelve. (Bergen Academies in New Jersey comprise another well-known cluster of technical high schools with high enrollment rates.[23]) Students can return to the comprehensive high school they would have attended at any time. The major requirements in Massachusetts for admission to its technical regional high schools are passing the state's grade-eight tests (these schools have complex and expensive equipment) and an interview. At least half the teachers are males, increasingly important role models for many boys today. Although the national dropout rate has been decreasing since 1967,[24] 40 percent of black males don't graduate from high school[25] and about 30 percent of black female dropouts are pregnant.[26] High school curriculum choice may serve to retain them until graduation.

Programs seeking to close "gaps," not to advance the academic achievement of all students. State legislatures can ban all programs seeking chiefly to close "gaps" on the grounds that they discriminate against some of the identifiable demographic groups in the state by not aiming to strengthen academic achievement in members of all groups.[27] If programs claim they do both, then they must provide credible evidence they do.

LARGE-SCALE PROGRAMS WITH EVIDENCE

1. The Massachusetts Education Reform Act of 1993 (MERA). It is the only comprehensive education reform bill that has ever been shown to be effective in strengthening public education for all students, to judge by state, national, and international tests. Among the many reasons for its effectiveness are

    a. its philosophy that it was in the public interest to increase academic achievement in all students (gap-closing was not its mission);
    b. its emphasis on upgrading the academic quality of the state's teachers and administrators (all new teachers had to pass tests of the subjects they hoped to teach;
    c. the development of first-class state-based K–12 standards to be used as a reference point in teachers' licensure tests, classrooms, professional development, and student tests; and
    d. the development of statewide tests of all major subjects, with test items vetted by the state's teachers, with cut scores determined in part by them, and with used test items made available to the public within a year or so of use.

2. Chartered schools with a strong and planned curriculum. For example, the Arizona-based Basis Charter Schools,[28] the New York City Success Academies,[29] and the KIPP Network of elementary, middle, and high schools.[30]
3. Schools that participated in the "NYC Core Knowledge Early Literacy Pilot."[31]
4. Massachusetts's regional career-technical high schools. A major co-author of MERA has recently commented on them.[32]

POSSIBLE LONG-TERM SOLUTIONS TO MASSIVE ADOLESCENT UNDERACHIEVEMENT

1. Centralization of educational policies for low achievers

    a. First needed are signed agreements from parents making their own low-achieving children education wards of the federal government, and giving the federal government legal authority to determine standards and tests for them in coordination with groups or organizations that Congress and parents believe should have a stake in their educational program. State legislatures also need to pass laws allowing the federal government to set pass scores for tests for education wards and specifying who these people should be. There is advice on how to set pass scores on the Foundation for Educational Excellence website.

b. Education wards are to be enrolled in federal programs paid for, staffed, and evaluated by federal personnel (but not the same people) appointed by elected federal officials.

c. If parents choose not to make their low-achieving children education wards of the federal government, then their children attend local public schools governed only by policies voted on by locally elected school boards and financed only by local and state taxpayers—not by any federal guidelines issued directly or by appointed staff at state departments of education or by any federal grants or programs. All policies affecting local K–12 public schools must be made by officials directly accountable to local voters.

d. Data collections are to be allowed only for children who are education wards of the federal government.

2. Policies designed to promote steady school attendance
3. Federal and state policies designed to promote stable two-parent families in annually evaluated programs
4. Disallowance of test-based gap-closing policies and programs in a state. State legislatures can mandate that all of a state's K–12 school programs/curricula are to be nondiscriminatory and show intent to advance or accelerate the academic achievement of all students qualified to participate in them, within the full range of choices to be made available to all parents
5. Provision of many more regional four-year career/technical high schools in each state, with voluntary enrollment
6. No high school diplomas awarded students unless grade-twelve students pass the Citizenship Test (used for naturalizing intending citizens). They should be given to those who want to become legal citizens as well as to those students whose parents are already citizens. Pass score is to be set by law by the state legislature

NOTES

1. Andrew Coulson, The Impact of Federal Involvement in America's Classrooms, testimony to Committee on Education & Workforce, United States House of Representatives, February 10, 2011, https://www.cato.org/publications/congressional-testimony/impact-federal-involvement-americas-classrooms.

2. Andrew Coulson, "State Education Trends: Academic Performance and Spending over the Past 40 Years," Policy Analysis (Washington, DC: Cato Institute, March 14, 2014), https://object.cato.org/sites/cato.org/files/pubs/pdf/pa746.pdf.

3. Mary Campbell Gallagher, "Lessons from the Sputnik-Era Curriculum Reform Movement," in *What's at Stake in the K–12 Standards Wars*, ed. Sandra Stotsky (New York: Peter Lang, 2000), 305.

4. E. D. Hirsch *Why Knowledge Matters: Rescuing Our Children from Failed Educational Theories* (Cambridge, MA: Harvard Education Press, 2016).

5. Michael Hansen, "Instruction, Culture, and Curriculum in E.D. Hirsch, Jr.'s "Why Knowledge Matters," Brookings Institution, October 25, 2016, https://www.brookings.edu/blog/brown-center-chalkboard/2016/10/25/instruction-culture-and-curriculum-in-e-d-hirsch-jr-s-why-knowledge-matters/.

6. "ESSA," Thomas B. Fordham Institute, n.d., https://edexcellence.net/policy-priorities/essa.

7. Career Readiness and the Every Student Succeeds Act: Mapping Career Readiness in State ESSA Plans—Round 1, n.d., Advance CTE and Education Strategy Group, https://cte.careertech.org/sites/default/files/files/resources/Mapping_Career_Readiness_ESSA_Round1_2017.pdf.

8. Paul Solman, "Are College and Career Skills Really the Same?," PBS NewsHour, June 14, 2013, http://www.pbs.org/newshour/economy/are-college-and-career-skills/.

9. Bill Duncan, "A Closer Look at Sandra Stotsky's Critique of Common Core Standards," November 10, 2013, https://anhpe.org/2013/11/10/a-closer-look-at-sandra-stotskys-critique-of-the-common-core-standards/. Duncan was appointed to the New Hampshire State Board of Education by then Governor Maggie Hassan, now one of the state's national senators.

10. Bill Duncan, "James Milgram's Dishonest Critique of the Common Core Math Standards," *Advancing New Hampshire Public Education*, January 23, 2014, https://anhpe.org/2014/01/23/james-milgrams-dishonest-critique-of-the-common-core-math-standards/. Duncan was appointed to the New Hampshire State Board of Education by then Governor Maggie Hassan, now one of the state's national senators.

11. Mark Bauerlein and Sandra Stotsky, "How Common Core's ELA Standards Place College Readiness at Risk," White Paper No. 8, Pioneer Institute, September 2012, http://www.schoolimprovement.com/docs/PioneerInstitute_CoreELARecommendations.pdf.

12. Liana Heitin, "E.D. Hirsch Jr. Calls for Knowledge-Based Curriculum, Criticizes Common Core," *Education Week*, October 11, 2016, http://www.edweek.org/ew/articles/2016/10/12/cultural-literacy-creator-carries-on-campaign.html.

13. Thomas Newkirk, *Postscript: Speaking Back to the Common Core* (Portsmouth, NH: Heinemann, 2013), https://www.heinemann.com/shared/onlineresources/e02123/newkirk_speaking_back_to_the_common_core.pdf.

14. Sandra Stotsky, "Were Common Core's ELA Standards written by Charlatans? Sure Seems So." *New Boston Post*, June 16, 2016, http://newbostonpost.com/2016/06/16/were-common-cores-ela-standards-written-by-charlatans-sure-seems-so/.

15. Marina Ratner, "Making Math Education Even Worse," *Wall Street Journal*, August 5, 2014, https://www.wsj.com/articles/marina-ratner-making-math-education-even-worse-1407283282.

16. Andrew Coulson, "The Impact of Federal Involvement in America's Classrooms," testimony to the Committee on Education and the Workforce, United States House of Representatives, February 10, 2011, https://www.cato.org/publications/congressional-testimony/impact-federal-involvement-americas-classrooms.

17. Jane Robbins and Karen Effrem, "Schools Ditch Academics for Emotional Manipulation," *The Federalist*, October 19, 2016, http://thefederalist.com/2016/10/19/schools-ditch-academics-for-emotional-manipulation/.

18. One may find references on this site (http://www.casel.org/guide/) and the list of advisors on this site (http://www.casel.org/csi-standards-advisory-committee/).

19. Richard Bisk and Mike Winders, "Lowering Math Standards Not the Answer," *Commonwealth*, April 26, 2015, https://commonwealthmagazine.org/education/lowering-math-standards-not-the-answer/.

20. Mark Bauerlein and Sandra Stotsky, "How Common Core's ELA Standards Place College Readiness at Risk," White Paper No. 8 (Boston: Pioneer Institute, 2012), http://www.schoolimprovement.com/docs/PioneerInstitute_CoreELARecommendations.pdf.

21. William Estrada, "Trump Reins in Federal Role in Education, Common Core," *HSLDA*, April 27, 2017, https://nche.hslda.org/docs/news/2017/201704270.asp?utm_source=WU%20email&utm_medium=email&utm_campaign=WU.

22. Martin Levine, "Gates Foundation Apologizes Once Again for 'Learning Organization' Missteps," *NonProfit Quarterly*, May 27, 2016, https://nonprofitquarterly.org/2016/05/27/gates-foundation-apologizes-once-again-for-learning-organization-missteps/ and Sandra Stotsky, "How Do You Sell Common Core Standards and Tests to Unwilling Parents? Hide Them," *New Boston Post*, April 19, 2017, http://newbostonpost.com/2017/04/19/how-do-you-sell-common-core-standards-and-tests-to-unwilling-parents-hide-them/.

23. Bergen County Academies, https://www.niche.com/k12/bergen-county-academies-hackensack-nj/rankings/.

24. High School Dropout Rates, *Child Trends*, https://www.childtrends.org/wp-content/uploads/2014/10/01_appendix1.pdf/, https://www.childtrends.org/indicators/high-school-dropout-rates/.

25. Joseph Williams, *Black Brains Matter: Why Are Graduation Rates So Low?*, Report to Schott Foundation, February 11, 2015, http://www.takepart.com/article/2015/02/11/black-brains-matter-why-are-graduation-rates-so-low.

26. Dropout Rates among Pregnant Teens, n.d., http://www.teenpregnancystatistics.org/content/drop-out-rates-among-pregnant-teens.html.

27. Joe Gelonesi, "Is Having a Loving Family an Unfair Advantage?," *Philosopher's Zone*, May 1, 2015, http://www.abc.net.au/radionational/programs/philosopherszone/new-family-values/6437058.

28. "BASIS Charter Schools is a network of tuition-free charter schools in the United States, with schools located primarily in Arizona, where it was founded in 1998." For news on the high performance of many of its high schools, see https://www.aol.com/article/news/2017/04/24/arizona-charters-lead-2017-best-high-schools-rankings/22053669/. For critical comment, see https://www.washingtonpost.com/news/answer-sheet/wp/2017/03/30/what-the-public-doesnt-know-about-high-performing-charter-schools-in-arizona/?utm_term=.f0c6fd928f07.

29. Monica Disare, "Eva Moskowitz Looks Back at Her Turn Away from District Schools, as She Plans for 100 Schools of Her Own," *Chalkbeat*, October 16, 2017, https://www.chalkbeat.org/posts/ny/2017/06/12/eva-moskowitz-looks-back-at-her-turn-away-from-district-schools-as-she-plans-for-100-school-of-her-own/.

30. "M50, As the KIPP Network Grows, Positive Impacts Are Sustained," Research Report, *Mathematics Research*, September 17, 2015, https://www.mathematica-mpr.com/news/kipp-i3-scale-up.

31. NYC Department of Education, Evaluating the NYC Core Knowledge Early Literacy Pilot, K–Grade 2 Results: Year 3, Research and Policy Support Group, March 2012, https://www.coreknowledge.org/wp-content/uploads/2016/12/CK-Early-Literacy-Pilot-3-12-121.pdf.

32. Tom Birmingham, "Voc/Tech Schools Are a Mass Success Story," op=ed, Pioneer Institute, Boston, February 8, 2017, https://pioneerinstitute.org/featured/op-ed-voc-tech-schools-mass-success-story/.

TEN

Policies to Reduce Adolescent Underachievement or High School Dropouts

This final chapter suggests several long-term policies that could reduce massive adolescent underachievement and the number of high school dropouts. If adopted, they would at the same time improve the regular public schools for all the low- and higher-achieving students attending them. Low achievers cannot be abandoned by any society; they need to be educated for informed and active citizenship—the purpose of public schooling.

As the dean of a prominent graduate school of education noted in an article published several years ago, "Schools are not the major cause of the achievement gap."[1] Classifying reforms into four categories (preschool, teacher, instructional, and standards-based), he further noted how ineffective most education reforms have been and how little improvement we have seen, regardless of type of reform.

It is understandable that the head of an education school didn't want to see reform efforts transferred to other institutions. (Schools were not the *major* cause but still *a* cause.) He still thought it worthwhile trying to reform schools, even if there is little to show for it after fifty years.

FIVE EDUCATION-ORIENTED POLICIES

The following education-oriented policies won't solve the problems underlying massive adolescent underachievement. But they can address some of the unintended negative consequences that policy makers created in the past fifty years trying to address low achievement.

1. Centralize Education Policies for Low Achievers

Congress should continue to centralize educational policies for low achievers but in an agency of its choice and only for those students whose parents want the federal government to be in charge of all aspects of their education. All interested parents (low-income or not) should be allowed to participate.

Centralized education policies need to work better than they now do (and to be constitutional). To ensure greater parental cooperation than at present, the parent(s) of an infant or low-achieving child (or underserved learner) must voluntarily sign an *agreement* to allow all aspects of their children's education to be determined by a central agency (such as but not necessarily the United States Department of Education, the Maternal and Child Health Bureau, or the Department of Defense).

Congress also has to designate the central agency that could legally provide as well as administer and evaluate a service-delivery program, such as those that now exist for unaccompanied minors, refugees, and human trafficking. The agency could contract out the delivery of its service to other entities, but vouchers or scholarships could not be used for the program because it would be a public program.

Parents would be able to end their child's participation in the program as easily as they now do with any private school a child attends. They would simply notify program officials and register the child in the public school he or she would otherwise have attended.

To centralize education policy-making authority for low achievers in whatever agency Congress decides upon (thus removing this authority from state governments), *signed agreements* are needed from parents. These agreements in essence make their own low-achieving children education wards of the federal government.

State legislatures also need to pass laws allowing the federal government (or a congressionally designated agency) to set pass/fail cut-off scores on federally mandated tests (whether or not for federal education wards) that may have public consequence and specifying what kind of people should set these pass scores. This has not yet occurred, so far as is known, but needs to take place to make pass scores on these tests valid.

Federal education wards are to be enrolled in federal schools paid for by Congress and in programs staffed and evaluated by federal personnel (but not the same people) and appointed by elected federal officials. These programs would be for preschool to grade twelve but might be otherwise similar to the "boarding schools" for "disadvantaged" secondary students, begun a decade ago by the French government.[2]

The growing controversy over data collection by the state and federal government could be easily ended. All Congress needs to do is vote to allow data collection only for students who are education wards of the federal government and in a federal, not state, "system."[3]

If parents chose *not* to make their children education wards of the federal government, then their school-age children would attend public schools financed only by local and state taxpayers. Their local public schools would be governed only by policies and regulations voted on by locally elected school boards and elected state legislatures, not by guidelines issued by Congress, USED, state departments of education, boards of education, or federal grants to state departments of education serving as pass-throughs to the public schools or other organizations. There are several benefits to such an approach.

First, it would restore the original purpose of the Elementary and Secondary Education Act (ESEA). In 1965, Congress intended to strengthen public education. It clearly did not intend to close unspecified achievement gaps or to weaken the K–12 mathematics and science curriculum with a "social justice" approach.[4]

Second, it would make it possible for parents, if they prefer, to educate their children in schools likely to be more responsive to them than their local public schools are at present under a state plan. This would constitute a new form of school choice.

Third, it would considerably clarify the issue of accountability. To what bodies are local schools accountable for the (approximately) 90 percent of the funding they now receive from local and state sources? What needs to be changed as soon as possible is the unconstitutional nature of four-year state (education) plans. At present, these plans have been formulated by a state's department of education and then approved by a board of education in the executive branch of government (but not necessarily the governor), and then approved by USED. They have not been approved by elected state legislatures and the elected local school boards in the state.

Congress needs to give USED (or whatever agency it designates) the legal authority it doesn't have at present to determine K–12 standards and tests for low achievers, or "underserved learners" as they are now being called. This determination should be done in collaboration with parents who have a stake in the education program the designated agency is in charge of.

The agency given legal authority for delivering a full education program for the students signed over to its jurisdiction would prepare an annual Accountability Plan for Congress (the appropriating body for the funds spent on this program). Such a Plan should also be prepared for parents of the children in the program.

It is important to note that USED does not have to be the legal authority in charge of the education of low-achieving students in the country. Legal authority could be vested in a newly created agency similar to an old Chancery Court in England (a specialized equity court). But in this country today it could operate out of the Department of Justice.

Here is how these courts are described in Wikipedia:[5]

> The Court of Chancery was a court of equity in England and Wales that followed a set of loose rules to avoid the slow pace of change and possible harshness (or "inequity") of the common law. The Chancery had jurisdiction over all matters of equity, including trusts, land law, the administration of the estates of lunatics and the guardianship of infants.

The court, or its representative, was authorized to make decisions about the child's upbringing and assets, with the understanding that the child's welfare was the guiding principle. Thus, the child was what would be described today as a "ward of the court."

Wikipedia also notes, "The English Court of Chancery . . . was dissolved in the 1870s, but the Chancery Division remains a separate branch of the English legal system and of the High Court of Justice to this very day." Legal scholars would be needed to help establish such a court if this is how Congress sought to establish legal authority for a central agency in charge of education policies for low-achieving students.

2. Design Policies to Promote Steady School Attendance

These kinds of policies require brainstorming by school superintendents or whoever has enacted them and can speak to their effectiveness. They can be designed best at the local and state level.

Productive attendance policies give students an incentive to come to school, as a well-known teacher, Rafe Esquith, found with ways he devised for schoolchildren to accumulate credits for use in the classroom. Esquith taught grade five for over twenty-five years at Hobart Elementary School in central Los Angeles.[6] Students in his classes (often selected by the other teachers in the school) could accumulate credits by coming to school every day, passing in assigned homework on time, and passing in corrected homework that had been passed back earlier with teacher comments. They used these credits to "buy" their own desks, seats, and textbooks at a nominal price.

There were additional ways to earn credits in Esquith's classroom. But these basic ways were available to all students, allowed students to accumulate credit for classroom needs, and were easily understood by the children's parents. Like their children, parents learned why more expensive desks/chairs were near the chalkboard in rows called Boardwalk and Park Place and why less expensive ones were at the back of the small classroom in which he taught (about thirty-five students annually) in rows called Baltic and Mediterranean. Bottom line: daily attendance was very high.

3. Provide More Career/Technical High Schools in Each State

Each state has only a small number of Career/Technical Education (CTE) high schools. State legislatures, with the help of local industry and Congress, can increase the number of regional four-year CTE high schools in each state, all based on voluntary enrollment after students complete grade eight and under the jurisdiction of their own elected school board (as regional CTE high schools are in Massachusetts).

Education researchers apparently did not advise the (publicly unknown) writers of the Every Student Succeeds Act (ESSA) on the demonstrated value of curriculum choice in high school when the bill was written. Students in Massachusetts's thirty regional CTE high schools have had almost a 100 percent pass rate on state tests for many years and higher graduation rates than students in "comprehensive" high schools in Massachusetts. There has been little attrition from grade nine to grade twelve, even though students can return at any time to the comprehensive high school they would have attended. Most CTE schools in Massachusetts also have waiting lists.

The major requirements for admission to a CTE regional high school in Massachusetts have been (1) passing the state's grade-eight reading test, mainly because these schools have complex and expensive equipment, and (2) an interview. Given such requirements, these schools cannot serve as "dumping" grounds for illiterate children.

Another benefit of CTE high schools in Massachusetts is that at least half the teachers are males, according to a survey taken about a dozen years ago, and they serve as increasingly important role models for many boys today. Although the national dropout rate has been decreasing since 1967,[7] more boys than girls drop out. Enrollment in a CTE high school might help to retain more boys until graduation.[8]

CTE high schools do not discourage postsecondary education; over one-half of the graduates of these high schools in Massachusetts have gone on to some kind of postsecondary education. See Pioneer Institute reports in the past decade on the state's CTE high schools.[9] Bergen Academies in New Jersey comprise another well-known cluster of technical high schools with a range of curriculum options and high postsecondary enrollment rates.[10]

4. Disallow Gap-Closing Policies, Programs, and Standards

State legislatures and local school boards can mandate that their K–12 school programs and standards are to be nondiscriminatory and show intent to advance the academic achievement of all students qualified to participate in them, whether over-served or under-served, and forbid use of gap-closing standards.

Gap-closing standards, in contrast to content-based academic standards, inhibit the design or proper functioning of programs intended to increase all students' academic achievement. Gap-closing standards may flatten or lower educational growth for higher achievers by making tests harder but not more academically demanding, or by reducing the academic demand in upper-grade standards so that lower achievers can eventually close an academic gap (also known as the "soft bigotry of low expectations"). Cut-scores may also be lowered so that most students pass (and gaps are then declared closed).

So far, no state or local school board has indicated exactly how it will close achievement gaps. Nor has the U.S. Department of Education. If parents want gap-closing standards (presumably they are now in all state plans for ESSA), that would be a local school board's decision after unconstitutional state plans are eliminated. By lowering expectations for all students, such standards become racist standards, especially if gaps are calculated between groups defined by race or national origin.

Test items and cut scores have to be controlled for gap-closing standards to work. A process in which relevant grade-level teachers work with the testing company to review and revise test items and, with parents, help to determine cut scores (pass/fail scores) is the best antidote for manipulable test items and cut scores. Other measures can address other kinds of possible test-score manipulations.[11]

If all students are taught by academically strong teachers to academically strong standards and curricula, the gaps won't close (as in Massachusetts). While both low and higher achievers rose in achievement, weaker Massachusetts students did not catch up to stronger ones. Over time, many did get to where stronger students had originally been with respect to scores on state tests.

Adolescents need a choice of the kind of standards they want to try to meet. And parents should be allowed to withdraw their children from bogus programs that claim all students will soon perform at the same level on tests that teachers have not created and that teachers, subject matter experts, and parents have not reviewed.

5. Do Not Award a High School Diploma Unless the Student Passes Tests Using Only Test Questions on the Original Citizenship Test for Naturalizing Intending Citizens

The award of a high school diploma is controlled by a state legislature's requirements, not USED's. These tests should be given to those who want to become legal citizens, as well as to those students whose parents are already citizens. This idea has already been floated several times by Robert Pondiscio at the Thomas B. Fordham Institute, as well as by others.[12] So far, states interested in this test are not using it or the test questions as is.

Pass scores on a "civics" test must be set by a state legislature after a review of the questions on it. The National Commission of the States reports that seventeen states are using test questions "drawn" from this test. That language should raise a red flag when no examples of "drawn" test questions are provided.[13] Legislators and school boards need to ensure that only the actual questions on the original test are on a civics test and accept no "revisions."

These recommended policies could lessen massive adolescent underachievement. They would, at the least, serve to make the public schools more responsive to the parents of the children in them, to the children themselves, and to the local communities. But they won't solve the problem of massive adolescent underachievement.

How can education policy makers be helped to understand that massive adolescent underachievement is not susceptible to solution by educational interventions, no matter how much money is allocated to the public schools? How can policy makers be helped to understand that it is damaging to all students' education to expect the wrong institutions (public schools and colleges) to keep on trying to solve the problem? Finally, what are the civic costs of an obsession with low achievement?

A NON-EDUCATION APPROACH TO A NON-TEACHER-CAUSED PROBLEM

In addition to implementing education-oriented approaches to reduce massive adolescent underachievement, policy makers need to design non-education approaches to what is not a teacher/school-caused problem, such as policies that promote stable two-parent families as the goal of regularly evaluated programs.[14]

The research is consistently clear: On average, children from two-parent families do better academically than children from single-parent families. This finding also turned up in a study by William Jeynes of information from over 20,000 African American and Hispanic high school students in the National Educational Longitudinal Survey (NELS) from 1988 to 1992.[15] In the past fifty years single-parenting has been on the rise in most demographic groups.[16] But since the 1990s, a majority of African American children have grown up in single-parent families.[17]

Policy makers could start addressing the central finding of the 1966 Coleman Report: Families matter more than teachers.[18] They could also address a well-known finding (mentioned in chapter 8) on the importance of a mother's literacy skills. A child's achievement depends greatly on the mother's academic achievement level. The U.S. National Institutes of Health found "that a mother's reading skill is the greatest determinant of her children's future academic success, outweighing other factors, such as neighborhood and family income."[19]

Non-education approaches to a non-education-caused issue (massive adolescent underachievement), as well as academically strong standards, can start strengthening public education for higher as well as low achievers, as ESEA intended. And they could do so without assuming that either (or any) group has a particular color or national origin.

NOTES

1. Andy Porter, "Rethinking the Achievement Gap," *Penn GSE Newsroom*, n.d., http://www.gse.upenn.edu/news/rethinking-achievement-gap.
2. Luc Behaghel, Clément de Chaisemartin, Axelle Charpentier, and Marc Gurgand, "Les effets de l'internat d'excellence de Sourdun sur les élèves benéficiaires: Résultats d'une expérience contrôlée," Working paper, Cambridge, MA: Abdul Latif Jameel Poverty Action Lab (J-PAL), 2013). This paper reports on an experiment with a boarding school (Internat d'Excellence) in Sourdun, France, for secondary students from "disadvantaged backgrounds."
3. U.S. Department of Education, "Statewide Longitudinal Data Systems," July 2009, https://www2.ed.gov/programs/slds/factsheet.html.
4. To understand what a "social justice" approach in mathematics education is, first listen to a short interview with the head of the National Council of Supervisors of Mathematics, https://www.youtube.com/watch?v=E-puPR_WkB0. Then read the description of a mathematics education course that gives participants academic credit at https://www.campusreform.org/?ID=9187. "'Teaching Social Justice through Secondary Mathematics' is a six-week online course designed by Teach for America and offered through EdX, which provides free online classes from top universities such as Harvard University, MIT, and Columbia University. 'Do you ask students to think deeply about global and local social justice issues within your mathematics classroom?' a course overview asks. This education and teacher training course will help you blend secondary math instruction with topics such as inequity, poverty, and privilege to transform students into global thinkers and mathematicians."
5. "The Court of Chancery," *Wikipedia*, https://en.wikipedia.org/wiki/Court_of_Chancery.
6. Howard Blume, "LA Unified Settles Lawsuit with Teacher Rafe Esquith," *Los Angeles Times*, September 13, 2017, http://www.latimes.com/local/lanow/la-me-edu-rafe-esquith-settlement-20170912-story.html.
7. "High School Dropout Rates," *Child Trends*, October 1, 2014, https://www.childtrends.org/indicators/high-school-dropout-rates/.
8. Joseph Williams, *Black Brains Matter: Why Are Graduation Rates So Low?*, report for Schott Foundation for Public Education, February 11, 2015. According to the sources for this report, 40 percent of black males don't graduate from high school, http://www.takepart.com/article/2015/02/11/black-brains-matter-why-are-graduation-rates-so-low.
9. See, for example, Alison L. Fraser and William Donovan, Filling the Skills Gap: Massachusetts Vocational-Technical Schools and Business Partnerships , White Paper No. 124, Pioneer Institute, November 2014, http://pioneerinstitute.org/featured/study-vocational-technical-schools-and-businesses-strengthening-the-states-economy/.
10. "Bergen County Academies Ranking," 2018, https://www.niche.com/k12/bergen-county-academies-hackensack-nj/rankings/.
11. See, for example, John Jacob Cannell, *How Public Educators Cheat on Standardized Achievement Tests* (Albuquerque, NM: Friends for Education, 1989), http://nonpartisaneducation.org/Review/Books/Cannell2.pdf.
12. Robert Pondiscio, "Let's Set a National Standard for Our Students—a Really Low One," *Atlantic*, April 9, 2013, https://www.theatlantic.com/national/archive/2013/04/lets-set-a-national-standard-for-our-students-a-really-low-one/274808/; and Robert

Pondiscio, "Don't Know Much about History," *U.S.News*, March 20, 2015, https://www.usnews.com/opinion/knowledge-bank/2015/03/20/states-requiring-civics-exams-in-high-school-are-on-the-right-track.

13. Hunter Railey and Jan Brennan, "The Civics Education Initiative 2015–17," Education Commission of the States, September 13, 2017, https://www.ecs.org/the-civics-education-initiative-2015-2017/.

14. Paul Peterson, "Racial Controversies Are as Misleading Today as They Were When the Moynihan Report Was Written," *Education Next*, March 4, 2015, http://educationnext.org/racial-controversies-misleading-today-moynihan-report-written/. Also see, for example, Susan Brown, "Marriage and Child Well-Being: Research and Policy Perspectives," *Journal of Marriage and Family* 72, no. 5 (2010): 1059–77, https://www.ncbi.nlm.nih.gov/pmc/articles/PMC3091824/?_escaped_fragment_=po=40.6250; "Chapter 3: Family," Brookings Institution, https://www.brookings.edu/wp-content/uploads/2016/07/Chapter-3.pdf.

15. William H. Jeynes, "The Effects of Black and Hispanic 12th Graders Living in Intact Families and Being Religious on Their Academic Achievement," *Urban Education* 38, no. 1 (2003): 35–57. Jeynes found that "[s]tudents with intact families and high levels of religiosity scored as well as all white students on most achievement measures and higher than their black and Hispanic counterparts without intact families or high religiosity."

16. Dawn Lee, "Single Mother Statistics," *Single Mother Guide*, September 18, 2017, https://singlemotherguide.com/single-mother-statistics/; Jennifer Wolf, "Single Parent Statistics," *The Spruce*, January 17, 2017, https://www.thespruce.com/single-parent-census-data-2997668.

17. James T. Patterson, "Moynihan and the Single-Parent Family," *Education Next* 15, no. 2 (Spring 2015), http://educationnext.org/moynihan-and-the-single-parent-family/.

18. Kimberly Howard and Richard V. Reeves, "The Marriage Effect: Money or Parenting?," Brookings Institution, September 4, 2014, https://www.brookings.edu/research/the-marriage-effect-money-or-parenting/.

19. U.S. Department of Health and Human Services, "Improving Mothers' Literacy Skills May Be the Best Way to Boost Children's Achievement," October 25, 2010, http://www.nih.gov/news/health/oct2010/nichd-25.htm. See also Jared Wadley, "Mothers' Education Significant to Children's Academic Success," *Michigan News*, November 10, 2014, http://ns.umich.edu/new/releases/22501-mothers-education-significant-to-children-s-academic-success.

About the Author

Sandra Stotsky is professor of education emerita at the University of Arkansas, where she held the 21st Century Chair in Teacher Quality. She served as Senior Associate Commissioner at the Massachusetts Department of Elementary and Secondary Education from 1999 to 2003, in charge of developing or revising the state's K–12 standards, teacher licensure tests, and teacher and administrator licensure regulations.

She served on the Common Core Validation Committee from 2009 to 2010 and did not sign off on Common Core's standards because they were not rigorous, internationally benchmarked, or research-based. She was also editor of the premier research journal *Research in the Teaching of English*, published by the National Council of Teachers of English, from 1991 to 1997. She has taught at the elementary, secondary, undergraduate, and graduate level, published extensively in professional journals, and written (or contributed to) several books.

She was appointed by Governor Mitt Romney to the Massachusetts Board of Elementary and Secondary Education in 2006 and served until 2010. She served in the Town of Brookline as a Town Meeting Member from 1984 to 1994 and as a Trustee of the Public Library from 1984 to 1999. She also served as president of the Brookline League of Women Voters from 1971 to 1973. She received her undergraduate degree in French literature from the University of Michigan, and her graduate degree in reading research and reading education from the Harvard Graduate School of Education in 1976.